THE ROAD LESS TRAVELED

23 LIFE LESSONS FROM THE TRAIL

BRAD "SHEP" SASSER

CONTENTS

Thanks to Michelle, Lane, and Meredith. They are the compass that always leads me home.

INTRODUCTION

"For I know the thoughts I think toward you, says the Lord, thoughts of peace and not of evil, to give you a future and a hope." Jeremiah 29:11 NKJV

Someone once said, if you want to make God laugh, tell him your plans. While I'm not sure about God's sense of humor, I am sure that many times the plans we have for our lives are much different than the grand design God has for our life. I was one of these individuals.

While I wasn't sure what I wanted to do, I felt pretty sure my life would revolve around South Alabama in some way. I enjoyed the churches I had worked with in Alabama, my family was there, and statistics showed that most people never moved further than 50 miles from their place of birth.

It was early 2011, and I was enjoying success as a youth pastor. This night we were very excited because a group of us were attending the yearly Speed the Light banquet. Speed the Light provides transportation and equipment for missionaries, both at home and around the world. This was a meeting where they fed us very well, and we got together with our youth leaders to set our fundraising goals for the year. We were excited to raise funds for missionaries, but this year would set in motion events that would change the course of my life.

"Twelve thousand dollars, that's more than we've given before. Yeah, I think we should go twelve thousand dollars."

I was concerned when Thomas McInerny threw this number out. I had faith we could raise it, but I also knew I'd been told to be sure I had a plan to raise what we pledged. Is this the Lord, or pride? We better have a plan before we sign off on this.

"How do you think we should go about raising twelve thousand dollars, T-Mac?"

"I've been thinking about this, I think we should do a walk. Like a long walk, across the State of Alabama. We could get people to pledge money per mile walked and raise most of the money."

There it was. The idea we needed, and with the stroke of a pen on a pledge card, my journey into the world of long-distance thru hiking was set in motion.

LESSON 1
THE POWER OF TWO

*And He called the twelve to Himself, and
began to send them out two by two, and
gave them power over unclean spirits.*

— MARK 6:7 NKJV

T he Sun was just beginning to rise as Thomas and I
watched my wife's car drive out of sight. We were
standing at the Mississippi/ Alabama state line, back-
packs loaded, ready to begin our walk across Alabama. It
had been around six weeks since Thomas had made the
suggestion of a walk to raise funds for Speed the Light.

The last few weeks were a whirlwind of support
gathering, trying to find comfortable shoes, and deciding
where to stay along the way. Thankfully, we were blessed
by family, and several churches, that gave us shelter
every night on this week-long walk. All that stood
between us and the Georgia line was two hundred and

ten miles and several unintended consequences that would teach us the power of two.

One thing you must be prepared for when walking across rural South Alabama is dogs, and I had a great fear of big dogs. This was precipitated by childhood trauma that is best left for another story. One thing was for sure- I did not like big aggressive dogs and was woefully unprepared for these encounters.

Another unplanned issue was the baking sun. In West Alabama, this was not a problem. West Alabama had large trees that provided shade near the sides of the road. Sunburned legs were not a problem there. However, Thomas normally worked the night shift and slept during the day. He had not been in the intense sunlight in many months. When we got to the wiregrass area, the flat farmland, there was no shade on the sides of the road. Tree lines were far from us, and Thomas was baking despite the sunscreen he applied.

Ah, the shoes. One thing I constantly tell new hikers- don't skimp on their shoes. It is much better to have an off-brand pack than off-brand shoes. If the blisters on your feet become overwhelming, you can't hike. Having proper shoes and socks is of utmost importance. Do you care to guess who went cheap on the shoes? I'll give you a hint, he wrote the words you are reading. Yep, this guy. What's two hundred ten miles in shoes never meant for this challenge. Shoes are shoes, right? You live and you learn, but for the walk across Alabama, I was in for a world of hurt.

The hills of West Alabama presented their own problems. We had grown up in the southeast corner of Alabama- we know nothing of the hills in West Alabama. All our knowledge indicated Alabama was flat, apparently, we did not do our homework. There were several grueling hills in West Alabama on US Hwy 84, our route across the entire state, not to mention the one thing neither of us planned for: the Jim Folsom bridge across the Tombigbee River.

The granddaddy of all unplanned hindrances we would encounter was the span bridge across the Tombigbee River. If you've ever driven in West Alabama, you know that logging is one of the main industries. The roads can be a non-stop blast of log trucks. We had been blown back from the roadway several times by the wind gusts of these large trucks and we faced a test; twelve hundred feet across this span bridge, with no shoulder, and the potential for multiple log trucks blowing us off the bridge. This was not the easy walk across Alabama either of us had planned.

We learned a lot about life on this walk across Alabama. For one, life isn't easy, things don't go as planned, you must trust the Lord, and it's much better to have someone, a friend, a pastor, a brother or sister in the Lord, by your side. Let me illustrate.

Since I was deathly afraid of big, aggressive dogs, Thomas decided he would take the lead if any dogs charged us. He had grown up with dogs and was an animal lover. I agreed this was an amazing plan, I would hide behind him in the event of a dog encounter. Several times I jumped behind him in fear of the loud bark, but the vicious dogs never materialized. We were blessed that in two hundred and ten miles we only had to deal with a couple of such instances.

Then, I developed a plan to help Thomas with his sunburn. I'm a good size guy, I cast a large shadow. I had Thomas walk on the inside of me, away from the sun and in my shadow as much as possible. This way we could relieve some of the discomforts he was feeling. Likewise, he thought of ways to keep my mind off my feet.

Due to my previously mentioned choice of shoes, I developed large blisters on my heels, between my toes, and on the bottom of my feet. To say my blisters had blisters would not be an overstatement. I was incredibly miserable. I credit Thomas with doing the best thing he could to take my mind off the pain. He decided to encourage me to do what I do best; I told stories non-stop for the last eighty miles or so. He made me talk, got me to tell old football stories, things he knew I enjoyed talking about, which took my mind off the discomfort. I'm so glad I had him with me.

In the West Alabama hills, we both learned that there were times when we would each need encouragement. Sometimes I would get down when it seemed like the hill wouldn't end, and Thomas would encourage me to take my mind off the large, taxing hill. Having a positive, encouraging person with you will always make the journey, no matter how hard, more bearable.

The Tombigbee River bridge. How can I fully describe this bridge? It was long, it was high, you had no shoulder, and you could feel it sway under you as traffic passed. I'm not afraid of heights if my feet are on the ground. I am afraid of heights if I'm on a roof or a bridge. We stopped short of the bridge to develop our plan. We would pray no log trucks passed at the same time, we waited until we could see there were none coming and hoped that would hold. I found that if I looked down at the back of Thomas' feet, I wouldn't freeze up. So off we went! Somewhere about halfway we had enough of the swaying bridge and ran for it. We looked a lot like the kids from the movie "Stand by Me" as we ran across the last couple hundred feet of the bridge.

A key element of the power of two is the relief we feel when we aren't having to suffer alone. Satan will often try and make you feel like you are the only person in the universe struggling with whatever you may be dealing with. Alienation is a tactic of the enemy. When you have someone with you in the middle of the struggle, you are still going through a hard thing, but at least you are not the only one going through this.

When we look to scripture, we see several verses that give us insight. Matthew 18:19-20 states, "Again I say to you that if two of you agree on earth concerning anything they ask, it will be done for them by my father in heaven. For where two or three are gathered together in My name, I am there in the midst of them." The Apostle Paul was aware of this principle, he always traveled with a companion. When he and Silas were thrown into a Phillipian jail, they began to encourage one another, worship with one another, and the place was shaken. Ultimately, a family found salvation and they found freedom.

There is great power in agreement. If any two of you agree on "ANYTHING" according to the will of God, it will be done. Do not try to face your struggles alone. Loneliness can be disastrous. God created Eve so that Adam wouldn't be alone. The Hebrew word translated "lonely" in the Old Testament meant "one who is solitary, desolate, forsaken, wretched. There is a deep sadness of the soul when we feel like we are without a friend, without a sounding board, without a helping hand. Having another person with you destroys the power of loneliness in your life.

Ultimately, we were created for communion and community. In the beginning, Adam and Eve had this with God, after the fall this changed, but our need for relationships with others, and communion with God is the same. The pandemic has threatened to alienate people from friendships and communities. Be sure you have a few people with you that will walk with you, encourage you, and believe in you.

LESSON 2
STEPS OF FAITH

So, he said, "Come." And when Peter had
come down out of the boat, he walked on
the water to go to Jesus.

— MATTHEW 14:29 NKJV

For years I had worked in ministry while struggling to find my place in secular employment. I often wondered if my struggle had something to do with lacking the faith to put all finances in God's hand. I had made one foray into full-time ministry, which lasted for about three weeks before a friend called and hired me to work for him. Since then, I have worked in accounting and most recently insurance. Other than the three-week period I was what they call bi-vocational, which a wise older pastor told me never means part-time anything, it's full-time at everything.

Insurance turned out to be a good deal for me and my

family. I attained employment with a prominent company in the area. The kind of company you retire from, the one you'd be crazy to leave, a place that provides financial security. Ah, security, the one word that has crushed thousands of dreams. I don't fault those who seek security, I just happen to be one of those wired differently. I wish we'd understand we have one life, one chance to chase our dreams, one chance to pursue the call of God. If you want to walk on water, you must get out of the boat named security.

To say that I identified as a dreamer would be an understatement. I would sit in my cubicle, and later my office, and wonder, "Is this what the rest of my life looks like?" Will I be here until I retire, spend a couple of years on a beach somewhere collecting seashells, then go to my grave in pristine condition? No, this couldn't be what God had planned for my life, but what did God have planned? I agonized over this thought.

I had spent time hiking the Appalachian Trail. After Thomas and I finished the walk across Alabama, I immediately Googled, "Long Distance Hiking" and the Appalachian Trail popped up. I started section hiking, traveling small distances over days or weeks. I met wonderful people during my hikes and recognized the need for more Christian witnesses on trial. I began to pray about this need, never dreaming where this prayer would take me.

However, when I settled for the security of the prominent job, I was told to put those dreams on the back burner. I'd need to be married to this new job for a while, and for two years I did just that. Here's the deal, dreams fade unless we do something about it. You've got to take the step into the unknown; that is not an easy step.

I remember driving to my bosses' office in late February 2019. I knew this was going to be one of the hardest days of my life. This was going to be the day I quit one of the finest jobs in the State of Alabama. I walked in, sat down, and announced that I was leaving to become a Missionary on the Appalachian Trail. My boss told me they were never going to believe it at the home office.

"Appalachian Trail Missions work, they've never seen that one on separation paperwork at the home office before."

I believe there are many more people who have dreams in their heart, but they've never been able to take the step of faith to make them a reality. No, I do not consider myself special. I should have taken the step much earlier in life. I wrestled with my decision, I wondered if we would be able to raise our budget required to do missions work. "Will we be able to pay our bills, sell our house, and feed the kids? What about health insurance? Can we travel from Georgia to Maine with two kids, and two dogs, living in a tent? Please, do not pin any roses on me.

One of the greatest hindrances to the step of faith is "analysis paralysis." As you can see, I'm guilty. We think about everything that could possibly go wrong, every possible outcome. I identify with a friend of mine who says his backup plans have plans. I imagine the disciples on the boat doing the same thing.

"There is a storm, I'm not getting out of this boat."

"What if that's not Jesus, what if it's a ghost?"

"I'm not that great a swimmer, I'm a tax collector, surely I will drown."

"Who in their right mind would jump out of a perfectly good boat."

I could go on with these possible excuses because I'm a great excuse maker. The problem is we are called to walk by faith, not sight, but we depend on the looks of the natural situation so often. Jesus said, "come." One man stepped over the railing of the boat and will forever be the only human, other than Jesus, to have ever walked on water.

So many people ask the question, "what if I sink?" The better question is, "what if you don't?" To quote an evangelist friend, "I'd rather be a wet water walker than a dry boat talker." God is tugging on the heart strings of dreamers and begging them to ask the question, "what if I don't sink?"

To quote John Greenleaf Whitter, "For all sad words of tongue and pen, the saddest are these, "It might have been." I sometimes allow my imagination to take over, and I had a recurring thought that pushed me to take the step of faith. I imagined standing before God and hearing him say, "you know you didn't do too bad, you raised good kids, gave money to missions, lived a good Christian life, but let me show you 'what might have been'." I imagined myself standing there watching my life play out on a screen, what it might have been if I'd been willing to take the step, quit the job, go pioneer a mission's work.

God is not looking for someone who has it all together, he is looking for someone willing to take the step. If you have been distracted by "analysis paralysis", then it is no accident you've come across this book. I'm here to tell you there is great freedom on the other side of the step, but you must take that first one. I had some ideas of what my future ministry could look like, but you will see God has taken us in directions, and to places we never dreamed.

As I left the bosses' office, back in February 2019, I vividly remember the song that came onto the radio as I pulled my car onto Ross Clark Circle in Dothan, Alabama. It was the Casting Crowns song, *Only Jesus*. I don't feel it's any coincidence that this song came on my radio at this exact moment. This was a little God wink, and I cried like a baby. Not because I was afraid of what was ahead, because I had taken the step, and was walking on water.

LESSON 3
THE LIGHTER PACK

*Come to me, all you who labor and are heavy
laden, and I will give you rest. Take my
yoke upon you and learn from Me, for I
am gentle and lowly in heart, and you
will find rest for your souls.*

— MATTHEW 11:28 NKJV

If you are going to hike you need to have the proper equipment, and this equipment comes in all shapes and sizes. First you need a backpack made for hiking. Then you need all the items that fill this pack, your tent, sleeping bag, ground pad, cooking pot, extra socks, the list goes on. What I found on my first trip to the Appalachian Trail is these items add up to a lot of weight.

Upon arriving at Amicalola Falls State Park in Georgia you have the option to check in and sign the register. You can also go over and weigh your pack. I took my pack over and hoisted it to the hook attached to a scale, forty-three pounds was the reading. As an inexperienced backpacker I didn't think forty-three pounds was that bad. After all, I'd wandered around my yard wearing this pack, and forty-three pounds wasn't all that heavy. It wasn't long before I concluded that walking around in Alabama and hiking in North Georgia were two different animals.

As you begin your hike from the parking lot at Amicalola Falls you travel a half mile uphill incline to reach the base of a six hundred plus step staircase. This winding staircase is straight up to the top of the falls. The half mile walk, with a forty-three-pound pack, causes my leg muscles to begin burning, and the sight of the staircase causes my stomach to turn. I remember thinking, this would be so much easier if I didn't have this heavy load on my back.

The steps were agonizing, I was glad to have my brother-in-law with me, at least I didn't have to suffer alone. The steps went up in flights and at every landing we took a break. I would lean my heavy pack back against the railing to take some weight off my back and shoulders. Over the years I have seen many people struggle up these steps, in agonizing pain, with an over-sized pack.

Once the steps were behind us, I remember thinking, "we have it whipped now." Only to realize that the steps were mild preparation for the North Georgia mountains we were about to encounter. I told my wife later that if she'd been waiting for me with the car I'd probably have quit after the steps and never set foot onto the actual approach trail. The burning in our legs got no better as we wound our way along the approach trail to Springer Mountain. I sparred with myself internally at the thought of continuing with this heavy pack for the duration of the week.

"How do people do this for six months," we wondered aloud at the end of the day.

For me the answer was simple. I've got to get a lighter pack, buy lightweight gear, and learn how to pack the weight better. Eventually I got my total pack weight down to around sixteen pounds not counting water. For me it was a simple process to enjoy hiking, I had to lighten the weight.

Many of us carry burdens. Some days it seems we will crumple under the pressures of life and its everyday demands. Sometimes we are going through difficult seasons and wondering if it will ever end. How can I handle this load I've been given? In Matthew chapter 11 Jesus tells us how to lighten our packs.

His first admonishment, to those that labor and were heavy laden, was to come to him. The Jewish people were weighted down by the requirements of the law, and the numerous additional requirements added by the Pharisees over the years. How could they be good enough? How could they be holy? In a spiritual sense, Jesus was telling them that to take him was to be released from the bondage of these requirements.

Likewise, when we struggle, become overrun by

worry, and stand under clouds of depression and doubt, we can come to the one who gives relief to our soul. When it feels like we can't take another step, give it to Jesus. When you have nobody to depend on, you can depend on Jesus. It seems oversimplified, but spend time in the presence of Christ, sit quietly in prayer, meditate on the word, and you will almost literally feel the tension leave, clouds fade, and relief come.

When Jesus says, "take my yoke upon you," he is giving them imagery of a team of oxen plowing in the field. One ox pulling the load alone would be under tremendous strain. However, when you bring in a second ox, together, the team can handle the load. There becomes a balance of weight shared between the two. Sometimes hiking partners will accomplish this by having one person carry the tent, and another carry the cooking system. If they are camping together, they can split the weight and lighten the load. If we know Christ as our Savior, we always have someone with us to share the load.

Jesus illustrates this another way in John 14:26. He says that he must go to the Father, but he wouldn't leave us comfortless, but the Comforter would come. The word Comforter, as mentioned here, means Paraclete in Greek. Paraclete means "one who is called alongside another." A great example of this is the extraordinary moment shared between Derek Redmond and his father in the 400-meter sprint Semi-Final during the 1992 Olympic Games in Barcelona, Spain. As Derek was running, he tore his hamstring mid-race. He got up and began to limp forward but had no chance of making the finish line in his condition. There was commotion in the stands as his father jumped the guardrail, ran onto the track, picked Derek up under one arm, and began to walk with him to the finish line. He "came alongside" his son and helped carry him across the finish line. Wow, what an amazing picture of how the Comforter comes alongside us, shares the load with us, and helps us through.

Perhaps you have been struggling with the heavy load of life. Like me when I started hiking, I had some things in my pack that didn't belong. I learned quickly what these unneeded items were and did not carry these things with me on future trips. Sometimes hikers will get a friend, or experienced hiker, to do a "pack shakedown." This means they will go through the items in your pack and tell you what belongs, and what should be sent back home or discarded. Part of getting a lighter pack is allowing Christ to "go through your baggage." What are you carrying that you should release? What burdens, hurts, pains, from the past are hindering you from enjoying your future because they are adding additional weight? Today is a great day to exchange your heavy pack for a much lighter one. Allowing Christ to come alongside, to share the load, and go through your pack, is the key to walking forward unburdened into his beautiful plan for your life.

LESSON 4
OUR GOD PROTECTS

The God of my strength, in whom I will trust;
My shield and the horn of my salvation,
my stronghold and my refuge; My Savior,
You save me from violence.

— 2 SAMUEL 22:3 NKJV

When you spend enough time on the Appalachian Trail you are bound to have interesting stories; the one I'm about to share is by far my most interesting story. Even seasoned trail veterans have listened to this story with wide eyed wonder. I'm very glad we pray over our trips and believe God is a protector, because this story could have had a vastly different outcome.

After we ascended the stairs in Amicalola, and spent several days hiking northbound across Georgia, running into inclement weather. People ask if I'm afraid of bears, or snakes, and I always tell them I fear cold and wet weather worse than anything. Being cold and wet will kill you before any wild animal.

On this day we found ourselves in a torrential rainstorm. After checking the radar, spending some time huddled in the Twelve Tribes bus (that's a story for a different day), and catching a ride with a crazy Appalachian Trail shuttle driver, we found ourselves on the doorstep of Wolf Pen Gap Country Store in Suches, GA. This was a gas station, with a hostel built over the top of it, in a sleepy little North Georgia town. As I got out of the shuttle driver's van, I listened intently hoping I didn't hear banjos playing. We were willing to stay anywhere dry on this night.

Occasionally, I have people ask me about hiker hostels so this might be a good time to describe them in general and try to paint a good description of this one. A hostel is a place where a hiker can rent a bed, and often get other services like showers, laundry, and resupply of food. Some may be private residences opened to hikers, others a bunkhouse filled with wooden bunk beds made for maximum capacity during busy seasons. Amenities vary, but one thing is for sure, the hostel at Wolf Pen Gap Country Store was not five star.

Imagine your local convenience store, the long ones that look like ranch style houses. Now imagine there is a staircase on the side of the building that leads to a large second story over the store. Once inside you have a communal area with a large couch right next to the door, a round kitchen table in front of the couch, and a kitchen behind the table. Down the hall there is a room on the right with about ten bunk beds, a single bathroom on your left, and a large room at the end with space for twenty bunks. These were wooden bunks with no mattress- I was not looking forward to sleeping on these. I figured the ground was more comfortable.

As luck would have it, I didn't have to sleep on the uncomfortable bunk. They overbooked the hostel due to inclement weather, and there weren't enough bunks. I hastily volunteered to sleep on the couch by the door. It was going to be a long evening, there were forty hikers and a bird dog in the hostel, and the young hikers showed no sign of slowing down. They played cards, heated pizza in the microwave, and tried to find quiet places to call their mother or girlfriends. I sat on the couch taking it all in, and that's when something strange happened.

Around eight o'clock that evening a young man appeared seemingly out of nowhere. I knew the store closed at seven and this fellow had arrived later than seven, so he was not a registered occupant for the night. I also noticed he wore dirty jeans, and a Carhartt jacket. This is another sign we weren't dealing with a hiker. All hikers know that cotton is a killer on the trail. It holds moisture, is cold, and won't dry easily. It gets very heavy when wet as well. Hikers opt for synthetic blends and dry fit material which is lightweight and dries easily. I made a mental note that I would keep an eye on this kid.

As the night wore on the weather seemed to get worse. I was glad we had made the right call to come to the hostel. Forty hikers, of all shapes, sizes, ethnicities, creeds, and a bird dog made for an interesting night with one bathroom, but at least I was dry. It was nearing midnight and the youngsters had finally started to head for bed. I was happy, my age was showing, and I was tired. The one thing keeping me awake was this odd young man who obviously wasn't a hiker. Where had he come from? What was his story? I'm an inquisitive person by nature, and I'm always interested in people's stories, but I hadn't made any headway getting this fellow to talk. He just sat in the corner and seemed to have a lot on his mind. I decided to reach out to him again and offer to let him share the couch, there was a recliner on both ends. I'd sleep on the side closest to the door, and he could have the other end. I figured this would help me keep an eye on him. The living area already had two young ladies from Wisconsin sleeping on the floor next to the table in the same room.

"Hey, why don't you sleep over here on the other end of the couch. These recliners kick out and make a good place to sleep."

"No thank you, I've been on a long journey, I think I'm going to sleep here on the floor," was his reply.

With that he placed a suitcase, not a hiking pack, a suitcase, next to the couch I was sitting on. Then he put a couple books he carried on the floor for a pillow and laid down next to the door. I turned off the light, and settled in for, what I knew would be, a long night. I listened as he shuffled around. I could hear snoring in the other bunkrooms, but I knew my friend by the door wasn't asleep. If he wasn't sleeping, I wasn't sleeping. Then he got up and began creeping around from room to room in the darkness. There was one small night light that illuminated enough of the hall I could see his outline. I started thinking, "he's going to kill us all." Then he came back and laid down with his books. I prayed silently asking the Lord to watch over us. After all, this was a dark and stormy night, all the scary movies started just like this.

I'd estimate I sat awake in the darkness listening to this guy breathe, hoping he'd drift to sleep, for about an hour. Finally, it seemed he'd settled in and went to sleep. Maybe now I could get some sleep; just as I was dozing off, I heard a car pulling into the gravel lot outside. Then I heard footsteps coming up the outside staircase. They sounded heavy, like big boots. I quickly reminded the Lord that I'd prayed he would watch out for us. Then, the door swung open.

Standing in the doorway holding a flashlight was a very large man. He wore military fatigues and had a well-formed beard. He shined the light in my face, shined it on the girls by the table, then finally shined it on the young man by the door. He proceeded to kick the kid's foot. This young guy jumped straight up at attention like he was in the military. The bearded man said, "You ready to go, get your stuff," in a deep voice. With that they both turned and walked out the door and down the steps. I'm telling you; this was possibly the second scariest moment of my entire life. What had I just witnessed? The two girls from Wisconsin suddenly started screaming that they thought he was going to kill us. Apparently, they had my same concerns about the young man and had laid on the floor awake as well. I quickly slid the couch over in front of the door and told them nobody else was getting in or out tonight.

This story sounds hard to believe, but it's true. For me it perfectly illustrates the protecting hand of God. I found myself in a situation that I was totally unprepared for, a situation that was outside my scope of control, but God is always in control.

Perhaps, no person in the Bible knew more about the protection of the Lord than David. In the title passage from 2nd Samuel, he is rejoicing in the fact that the Lord was his shield, his rock, his stronghold, his refuge, his Savior, and his God. If we know the Lord, we too can rejoice in this. God is not some far away distant deity, but he is our constant companion, and closest friend. Proverbs 18:24 tells us there is one who clings closer to us than a brother. Rejoice in that!

David knew the Lord was a protector because he has experienced this repeatedly in his life. God protected him from the lion and bear, as a Shepherd boy, long before he delivered him in the fight against Goliath. God protected David in the highs and lows of life. From the throne of a king to a life on the run from his own son. Likewise, on the trail I have experienced the protection of the Lord in many circumstances.

Once while hiking in Pennsylvania, I almost stepped on the largest rattlesnake I had ever seen. Pennsylvania is notorious for these snakes in the woods due to the large number of loose rocks they can hide under. Some hikers call Pennsylvania, Rocksylvania, because of the amount of rock. This particular day I was strolling along, trying to catch up with a group that was just ahead of me. I heard another hiker behind me and turned to say hello while still moving forward. When I turned back around and looked at my feet I was stunned. There was a large rattlesnake curled up next to my foot, rattles shaking. I jumped, a jump that would have made Lebron James feel good. The other hiker and I watched as this snake uncoiled and crawled off trail. No doubt I said a prayer right there thanking the Lord. That was close and we were about five miles from the nearest road.

Sometimes we become disheartened because we equate God's protection to freedom from problems. Please refrain from doing this. Jesus actually promises we will have problems in John 16:33. If the Christian life were going to be free of trouble then what is to be said for Job, and the Apostles which suffered a martyr's death. The oft quoted Isaiah 54:17, says "No weapon formed against you shall prosper." However, it doesn't say you will not receive attacks, you will be free of trouble, or worrisome situations. It says you will not be struck by the weapon. It would be nice to be saved FROM the fire, and FROM the lion's den. That is usually not how God works. In those situations he received the ultimate glory from saving them Hebrew boys, and Daniel, in the midst of their trouble.

One more story about the Lord's protection. When you've been in the field long enough you have a lot of these stories. I was recently driving up interstate 81. Due to the mountainous terrain, there are only a couple routes north through Virginia. I-81 is the preferred route for most truckers, combined with the auto traffic, this creates a bottleneck in central Virginia. The Friday before Thanksgiving I found myself in one such bottleneck. I would later learn that the universities along I-81, including Virginia Tech, had just let out for the holiday; this led to an influx of cars, meshing with holiday traffic, big rigs, and people like myself who had no clue about the traffic. Suddenly, as I drove, the cars ahead of me began locking up their brakes, something akin to a NASCAR wreck in turn four was happening just in front of me. With no time to react I remember glancing in my side view and rear view, I had nowhere to go. I locked up the brakes, dodged left off the interstate, felt the backend of the truck break loose and I began sliding sideways coming to rest with a thud as my rear end smashed into a gravel and dirt embankment. I sat still for a moment, waiting to feel pain- there was none. I glanced around at other drivers now scattered around, no single car had any major damage. I remember thinking this was unbelievable. It defied reason that I did not T-bone the little red car ahead of me with the Alpha Gamma Delta sticker on the back. How did we all get out of that without a scratch on a person? Another driver, a man from West Virginia, pulled over to talk with me.

"Man, I've seen it all. I don't know how you missed them; I don't know how you didn't flip. Craziest thing I've ever seen"

Well, it was the craziest thing I'd personally ever been through in an automobile. I ended up needing a tow from the roadside to get me out of the hole. The small dent in my bumper was all I had to show for the scary ride. Was God protecting me that day on I-81, you bet he was, and my new friend from West Virginia agreed, "that was the hand of God alright."

We are all either about to go through a time of needing God's protection, in the middle of a situation currently, or just came out of a situation and preparing our heart for the next one. This cycle is just life in a fallen world. I challenge you to look to your helper, your rock, your shield, and your fortress. Remember what he has done for you and know he will do it again. The final part of John 16:33 says, "for I have overcome the world." Even though we may have troubling situations arise, the one next to me will bring me through. Rejoice!

LESSON 5
NEVER STOP LEARNING

Give instruction to a wise man, and he will
be wiser; Teach a just man, and he will
increase in learning.

— PROVERBS 9:9 NKJV

I f we ever think we've come to the place of arrival, that we know it all, we've learned all there is to learn, we fool ourselves. There are so many things to learn, and the Appalachian Trail is a great teacher. It's always fun to listen to inexperienced hikers talk in North Georgia. They have the same swagger and bravado we all had in eleventh grade. The equipment is nice and new, boasting of the training hikes back home, the jobs they left, their vacations in tropical climates, and their gear research. Some think they will hike the trail in under 100 days which is quite a feat. I laugh to myself when I'm around these hikers, I was one once myself.

I think back to all the lessons I've learned. The lack of proper shoes on my Alabama hike. I have hiked many miles since and have never gotten another blister while hiking. I've had the occasional hot spot, or tinder area, but never anything to match the blisters from that Alabama walk, because I learned a very painful lesson. I know now there is no need for multiple changes of clothes when you hike. My first pack weighed heavily partly due to having a change of clothes for every day, but I'll let you in on a secret I've learned, hikers don't change clothes very often. The time to change your current shirt is when your old shirt falls apart. You just wear it for a week straight until you get to the hotel bathroom, and you wash it in the sink. Then you wear it for two weeks until you get to a hostel, and they do laundry for you. The hostel will give you a loaner shirt until yours are dry. I know this sounds foreign, but I'm pulling the curtain back for you. After almost dehydrating, I learned you need to drink at every stream you come to if you're in an area that's slack on water. Even if you have plenty in your bottles. You may have to pee a lot later, but it beats dehydrating. The lessons go on and on. The key is learning from every lesson.

If we don't learn we are destined to repeat the same behavior and go through the same pain over and over. I don't know about you, but I'm allergic to pain. I will admit I've not always been the fastest study when it comes to learning life lessons. I'm hardheaded and strong willed, I've held onto some cards long past the point I should have folded, I don't like to admit when I'm wrong. Which my wife will tell you is almost never because I'll never admit it. I'm still a work in progress, but I'm learning.

My first snippet of advice is this: Find someone older and wiser than you and learn everything you can from them. How is it that I've never had another blister hiking? I listened to the advice of someone older and wiser. I had a gentleman in my church that was retired from the Army. I was telling him about my blister issue, and he gave me the fix. He told me in the Army they had to do long ruck marches with heavy packs. The key was making sure your feet stay dry by changing socks regularly, and pantyhose. Yes, knee high pantyhose. You cut them low and put them under your socks. They make a false layer of skin and create less friction than socks. You can buy liners in hiking stores, but they cost you around twenty bucks for a pair. The cheap knee-high pantyhose come with something like four pairs for five dollars, you be the judge. Two things I know, you will get some strange looks when you and the guys you are hiking with go buy knee high pantyhose, and this was great advice.

Trust people who have been down the road you are traveling, who have experience in the area. It's no secret I had a turbulent patch for a portion of my life when I was younger. Some people call it sowing wild oats, the problem is you'll spend the rest of your life praying for crop failure. I'm thankful for the older, wiser people God placed in my life, the ones who didn't give up on me, prayed for me, and patiently guided me through this time. Now that I've got gray hair, I'm happy to share with others who are walking down this same road. Hopefully, I have some good advice for wayward youngsters.

Another secret to learning is to experience the advice. We really don't learn until we put what we know into practice. You can tell me the pantyhose trick works, but until I go hike for days, and hike blister free, do I really believe you? Part of learning is to know; the other part is to do. Imagine an artist who has gone to school and studied, has all the brushes, and paints, knows the techniques of the masters, has the blank canvases, but never put the brush to canvas. It's not enough to know it, you must live it.

As Christians we have the tendency to fall into similar patterns. We learn the word, can quote scripture, have Bibles on shelves, but do we put what we know into practice. The word says love your neighbor, forgive your enemies, bless those that curse you, and turn the other cheek. Scripture also lists things God hates, things like lying, wicked imaginations, and sowing discord among the brethren. We are quick to excuse "common" sins while magnifying sins that don't hit as close to home. James 4:17 says, "Therefore, to him who knows to do good and does not do it, to him it is sin." This jarring statement by James takes the Christian life up a step. It's not enough to avoid evil, we must engage in the active pursuit of good. Everyday putting our faith into action. It's not enough to know it, we must live it.

Finally, let's understand that we can learn from anyone, and any situation. By anyone, I mean people who don't look, dress, or act just like you. I believe I can learn more from people who are less like me. One problem with living in a small town, and never traveling very far, is your only conversations, or life experiences, have been with people just like you. Perception is reality. The way you perceive the world around you affect the way you live, creates misunderstandings, irrational fears, and prejudices. I'm from South Alabama, until I was twenty-five years old the farthest, I'd traveled from home was Little Rock, AR, I'm an expert about narrow-mindedness. Mark Twain has a great thought on this matter. He said, "Travel is fatal to prejudice, bigotry, and narrow-mindedness, and many of our people need it sorely on these accounts. Broad, wholesome, charitable views of men and things cannot be acquired by vegetating in one little corner of the earth all one's lifetime." I'm thankful for friends and travel who challenge me to think deeper and push me to greater understanding of the human condition, greater sympathy, and greater compassion.

It's very easy to sit in your little corner of the world and look at everything around you with a judgmental glare. It's easy to share memes on social media degrading every lifestyle your politics or preferences seem to mandate. The hard thing is to sit down at a table, or a campfire, and have a conversation with someone completely different than you. To see your preconceived notions crumble, to feel compassion, empathy, and understanding. To walk away realizing perhaps some things you thought were true, are false, and forbid, you learned from the experience. I'll share a story.

I tend to spend lots of time at certain hostels. At one

hostel I met a brother and sister, I could tell they were struggling with life, and came hiking as a reprieve. The Lord used a bad situation to allow me to spend lots of time with them one night. I'd never had a kidney stone, I'd heard it was the equivalent of a male giving birth, I wanted no part of this. One night as I rolled over in my tent, around 1:30 a.m., disaster struck. I felt like I had a knife twisting in the lower part of my back, I got up and started walking around, doubled over in pain. I stumbled from the woods over to the campfire, this sibling pair were awake talking. They advised me to drink water, so I sat and drank, and hurt, and drank some more. Eventually, around 6 o'clock in the morning, I passed the stone.

I learned this duo was from up north, Vermont. They were hiking out early the next day, but I told them I planned to set up about twenty miles away, I hoped to see them again. We had talked that night about my work, that I was a Chaplain ministering to hikers. I could tell the young lady got a little quiet, but nothing was said. Two days later I was set up, cooking lunch for hikers near Shady Valley, and the duo appeared. I got them food, and we sat down to hangout, they were the only hikers with me at that moment. Then the young lady said, "I just want you to know that you don't want to be nice to me. I'm a lesbian, and I'm struggling with addiction, I'm not the kind of person you're looking for, I'm out hiking trying to stay clean." I was startled by her frankness but respected her honesty. I told her, "You're absolutely the type of person I want to be nice to. I really enjoyed talking with y'all the other night, and you guys helped me through that kidney stone ordeal. I'll help you anyway I can"

What we need to realize is Jesus' go to was love, he led with love. His first response to those in need was love. When someone is hurting, they don't need another, "I told you so," or another sermon. What they need is a hug. They need respect, sympathy, and understanding. This is not something I grew up knowing, this is something that I've learned.

My new friends and I were in tears before lunch was over. Imagine, a preacher, and a struggling addict sitting under a tree eating lunch, sharing stories, crying our eyes out. We prayed, they hiked on, both of us richer for the time we spent together. I sat under that tree for a good while, trying to process what I'd experienced, thinking about how far God has brought me. Praying for my new friends. Yeah, it's easy to beat someone up because they live differently, but I encourage you to sit under a tree and cry with them sometime. You never know what you'll learn.

Proverbs says teach a man, and he will increase in learning. I hope we all find mentors, older and wiser to learn from, that we put what we learn into practice, and that we understand how much we can gain from someone who doesn't think just like we think.

LESSON 6
DO THE UNEXPECTED

*But do not forget to do good and share, for
with such sacrifices God is well pleased.*

— HEBREWS 13:16 NKJV

Several years ago, I sat down with a group of missionaries to eat lunch with a former missionary. He was there for us to ask questions, bounce around ideas, and generally share his knowledge. He talked with us for about two hours, but one thing he said has stuck with me and I've never forgotten it. He simply said, "If you do the unexpected, you'll never be forgotten." Wow, such a simple nugget of advice that has pinged around in my head from Alabama to Maine, but the best advice is meaningless if we don't put it into practice.

I was calculating the cost of items in my buggy as I hurried around the aisles. "Man, why does all this trail blessing food have to be so expensive," I thought to myself. You see, feeding hikers is one of our main outreaches. We set up and cook hotdogs and hamburgers with all the fixings, chips, and drinks, from Georgia to Maine, at road crossings along the trail. This allows us to build relationships with hikers and ultimately gain the ability to speak to any issues and needs they have. I always struggle with balancing the two competing worlds of, "no cost is too much to help a hurting soul," with the real-world struggle of, "how much is in the budget for trail blessing food this month."

I was smack in the middle of this internal dilemma when it occurred to me, I had left a particular group of hikers out, and this was the expensive group. If you've never dealt with buying healthy food, in this case burgers and hotdogs for vegetarians, I can tell you it's more expensive. With this in mind, I knew I couldn't leave them out. They make up a small portion of the people we meet, and honestly, I know the Lord always supplies our needs. I put away the worldly thoughts of dollars and cents and grabbed a couple packs of veggie burgers and plant-based hotdogs. I pride myself on everyone having a seat at my table; I'm not going to leave this passionate group out. I knew that sometimes hikers with alternative food needs were forgotten, and while I can't meet every need, I was determined to do what I could.

I drove my truck up the winding forest service road outside of the little town of Nantahala, NC. I had two huge coolers, one loaded with water, soda, and Gatorade. Another is filled with hamburgers, and hotdogs, both vegetarian and non-vegetarian options. Then there was the flat cast iron griddle, along with the chips and buns. All the makings for a great day filled with big smiles, full bellies, and great conversations. As I pulled up, I realized I am alone, no other Trail Angel- the term hikers reserve for people who offer goodwill on the trail- is around. This will be a good day.

This location is at the bottom of a hill around a small bend in the trail. It's always encouraging to see the happiness on the hikers faces as they see you on the way down. This day started fast; three hikers came down the hill before my first table was set. I began handing out snacks and heating up the griddle. In no time I was surrounded by ten hungry hikers and was cooking hamburgers as fast as I could put them on the grill, and then it happened.

I noticed a young lady sitting to the side, eating an apple from the table, but nothing else.

"Would you like a burger, I asked?"

"No thank you, I don't eat meat."

"Well today is your lucky day, I thought I might have some vegetarians and I have veggie burgers."

She happily examined the veggie burger, and excitedly proclaimed this was the nice ones with real vegetables, not the fake processed stuff. I knew enough from my vegetarian friends to realize you needed to spend a little extra to get the real veggie burgers. After cleaning one side of the griddle, trying to get as much regular grease off the griddle as I could, I slapped them on. My first happily fed vegetarian hiker of the day. In total I fed around sixty hikers that day, four of them were vegetarians. One told me that she had missed out on several rounds of goodies earlier on the trail because there was nothing for vegetarians. She went to Instagram and tagged me in a post recounting the amazing day she had and the trail angel "Shep" who supplied veggie burgers. I saw her several more times throughout the year, and each time she excitedly talked about those veggie burgers.

Everyone should know there is a great big world outside your door just waiting for you. People are waiting for you to do unexpected things, to share your abundance, and to overcome negativity with love and kindness. Do the unexpected. The book of James contains one of my favorite verses, James 1:27, "Pure religion and undefiled before God and the Father is this, to visit the fatherless and widows in their affliction, and to keep himself unspotted from the world. (NKJV) So often we view our relationship with God as inwardly focused. That's keeping yourself unspotted from the world, but too many Christians stop there failing to realize that's only half the verse. The first part, a very important aspect of God's nature, is caring for the "fatherless and widows." Some read this as caring for one, the fatherless, and two, Widows, but that's the end. I believe the fatherless and widows were never meant to be exclusive categories, but examples of the needy. We were never to exclude anyone in need. A stranger, an illegal migrant worker, a drug addict, the homeless, our list goes on. To help the hurting around you, and to live in a Christ Like manner, that is religion. The writer of Hebrews equates doing for others and sacrifice, literally doing good for another is an act of worship.

In his book *Conspiracy of Kindness*, Steve Sjogren says that for centuries Christians have been known for many things. For wearing crosses, having certain hairstyles, wearing certain types of clothes, eating, or not eating specific things. But what is the one thing Jesus said his followers should be known for? That one thing is love.[1] John 13:35 says, "By this all will know that you are my disciples, if you love one another." (NKJV) In a world where people feel little love, you will be amazed at the doors that open when we reach out to show we care. The little unexpected things we do.

We often make mental notes of things hikers tell us. Some will say things like, "I'd do anything for fresh lemonade, or a fresh cucumber would be an awesome snack. We make our notes and try to have these things with us when we are in an area where we might see those hikers again. Imagine talking to a stranger in North Carolina, who cooked a burger for you, and offered you a drink. You mention your favorite drink is Peach Nehi. A month later you see these happy strangers again and they have your Peach Nehi. I have seen hikers sit and cry, overwhelmed that someone they barely knew would go through the trouble of having their favorite snack waiting on them two hundred and fifty miles later.

I do believe small acts of kindness, giving from our abundance, is an act of worship, and can change the world. I have seen small, unexpected acts of kindness tear down walls that have existed in someone's life for years. I challenge you to look for opportunities to do unexpected things for co-workers, for your spouse, and for complete strangers who can do nothing for you. These unexpected acts are seeds sown for the kingdom, and they'll never be forgotten.

LESSON 7
COMMUNITY OF KINDNESS

*So, continuing daily with one accord in the
temple, and breaking bread from house
to house, they ate their food with glad-
ness and simplicity of heart, praising God
and having favor with all people. And
the Lord added to the church daily those
who were being saved.*

— ACTS 2:46-47 NKJV

I wasn't sure what I was seeing the first time I laid
eyes on the Pioneer Village set up in the middle of
the woods. They had tried to describe this to me, but
traveling back in time two hundred years in a few
seconds will catch you off guard. I parked my truck,
unseen, in a wooded area near the setup and hurried
over to check this out.

The Frontier Camping Fellowship is a special

program of the Royal Rangers which allows boys to develop special skills, learn a more primitive way of life, and enjoy the spirit of adventure exemplified by early explorers. They wear period correct clothing, and sleep in the canvas tents of the Frontier Village. Each member selects a different type of buckskin and clothing based on a particular trade that they have selected from the time. Imagine seeing a trapper, a blacksmith, and a hunter working together to build firepits, hang cast iron utensils, and set up canvas tents. This is a special experience when set up in any location, but one that seems remarkably at home in the wilderness of the North Carolina mountains.

Men and boys scramble in the late afternoon sun. It's Thursday evening and the goal is to be set up by sundown to welcome hikers into the village early Friday morning for breakfast. A tent is set up to house the cook stoves, both chili and lentil soups are on the menu- lentils for our vegetarian friends. Another tent is the main gathering area with a fire for warmth, and coals are shuffled from this fire down to the Dutch oven cook space. Biscuits and sausage patties are cooked in these Dutch ovens. Finally, the sleeping tents are arranged near the main gathering tent. The finished product looks like a picture from a Lewis and Clark movie.

I could smell the sausage cooking when I rolled out of my tent. I typically sleep up, or down the hill away from the village. My tent is a regular hiking tent, and I don't want to infringe upon the hard work the Rangers have put into making their village pristine. The sun was just appearing over the mountain to the east; what a beautiful day. It takes some time to get the Dutch ovens up to speed in the cool spring weather. Wood is burnt and then coals are placed over and below the ovens to cook the biscuits and sausage. It wasn't long and the first hikers appeared from the woodline.

"What is this?"

"Wow, what have we stumbled into?"

The hikers happily wondered aloud as they took off their packs and headed over to the hand sanitation area. The young bucks, that's what the young Rangers are called, work the entrance table filled with fruit, candy, boiled eggs, and other goodies. Then, they send hikers over to take the packs off and get some food. Many hikers are overcome with emotion when they see the plethora of food and drink. They simply can't believe that someone would go through this much time and trouble just for them.

There are numerous wooden chairs sitting around the fire where hikers can warm up, grab a bowl of chili, some soup, and perhaps best of all, a sausage biscuit. Hikers are welcomed into this community of believers, a group that has created a special space just for them. Curiosity overwhelms hikers and many questions are asked.

"What is this group called?"

"Where are you from?"

"Do you guys care if I take pictures, they're never going to believe this back home?"

The men, boys, and a few wives who made the trip,

all dressed in their Frontier Camping attire, smile for pictures. For many hikers this will become a special story to be shared with others down the trail. It is not unusual for a hiker to spend an hour or more around the Ranger fire. As the sun begins setting, and chances of making big miles wanes, hikers from the first day will set up camp near the village. Why keep hiking when some of the best food on trail is right here? The night falls and the village has expanded to include several more tents, hiking tents, filled with very full and happy hikers.

I've had a few special stories come from this event. One that sticks out to me is a fellow named Wiley. Wiley was hiking alone when he came down the hill to the Pioneer Village. This fellow was burly, long ponytail, intricate tattoos, hands that looked like he'd seen many years of hard work. He sat quietly and ate his fill of biscuits and chili.

Before hikers leave, someone in the group tries to uplift them, tell them best wishes on their journey, and if the Lord leads, pray for them. I saw Wiley slipping off to his pack and reading the pamphlet the Rangers prepared with their favorite verses. Each hiker is given a pamphlet. I went over to speak, and tears were running down the cheeks of this big, burly, bearded hiker. He told me he'd never felt love like he felt here in this setting. People doing good for others, without desiring anything in return. I explained that we were sharing the love of Jesus, just showing love in very practical ways, a bowl of soup, a biscuit, a friendly smile, an offer to have prayer. I prayed with Wiley, and he went on his way northbound.

Interactions like these don't happen unless we intentionally create communities of kindness and action. I believe we are called to enjoy the company of others. Part of God's plan for humanity was community. In the book of Acts, the beginning of the church, a large part of the lives of believers was their community. They broke bread together, shared things in common, helped widows and orphans, in other words they took the commands of Christ to heart.

One way community exists is belonging to a local body of believers. Inside of this community we see the needs of others around us more clearly. Likewise, when we have needs arise in our own lives, we know that others are there to stand with us, pray for us, offer support and council. We are each given specific roles inside of the body, when our strength combines with the strength of another, we realize we are a part of something very special, something greater than ourselves.

The great danger for the local body of believers is to be perceived as an exclusive club for the high and holy. To create communities of kindness, the type of churches that make a difference, we must be able to project the beauty of the local assembly outward for the world to see. Yes, we share love towards the person across the aisle, and we should go outside and share that same love with the drug addict across the street. We invite our best friend at work to come sit with us on Sunday morning and enjoy service, but we should also invite the homeless man at the gas station we walk by every week. One of my favorite Pastors is Jim Raley. I would say I listen to him at least once a week online. Pastor Raley once said God told him, "If you will take care of the ones nobody wants, I'll send you the ones everybody wants."

It is so easy to love people who look just like you, think like you, dress like you. We are not afraid of people we are comfortable with. But, to fulfill the Great Commission, we must create communities that love the unlovable, that love the have nots, and the not yet. Too often we force people who don't look, or think, like we do toward the edges, sometimes unknowingly, sometimes not. Remember the words of Jesus in Matthew 22: 37-39, "Jesus said to him, 'You shall love the Lord your God with all your heart, with all your soul, with all your mind. This is the first and great commandment. And the second is like it: You shall love your neighbor as yourself.'" (NKJV)

So, there is the challenge, to create environments, in our churches, in our homes, that show and share the love of Christ. Then, figure out ways to take this love outside the walls of traditional church, to the world. Remember the Great Commission said, "Go and tell," not sit and wait. We need to create a loving community for those that come, but also plan to take the Gospel out to those that never would. The world is full of people like Wiley, who have never experienced the love of Christ, never had someone give of their abundance expecting nothing in return.

LESSON 8
DON'T QUIT ON A BAD DAY

In the day of prosperity be joyful, but in the
day of adversity consider: Surely God has
appointed the one as well as the other, so
that man can find out nothing that will
come after him.

— ECCLESIASTES 7:14 NKJV

On the Appalachian Trail hikers have a saying, "Don't quit on a bad day." Anyone who has spent time in the terrain, and weather, of the Appalachian Mountains has experienced this saying firsthand. I can attest, you don't camp for weeks with two kids, and two dogs in a tent, without experiencing these days. One of those times happened on our first trip to Pennsylvania with the family.

We camped for several days in the beautiful Northern

Virginia town of Winchester. It was early July, and the summer storm season was very active. We had a large tent that held our family of four, plus our dog Bella. After a week of on and off severe storms we packed up wet gear and headed for Pine Grove Furnace State Park in Pennsylvania. We assumed the wet gear was the worst of our worries.

We arrived at the park and got our lot assignment. I had no clue what the campground looked like, you made reservations online and were assigned campsites with no prior knowledge of your site. All we were told was watch out for sites near the dumpsters because there might be bear activity. The park told us we'd be in campsite 36; while I love this campground, we learned, you do not want campsite 36.

Pulling up we could see that this site was not made for a tent. There was no tent pad on the site, just packed gravel for a travel trailer. I told my wife Michelle, "maybe we can make it work," we'll just try and put the tent sideways on the small patch of grass between us and the neighbors. Now it was starting to rain, great.

I tried to drive the tent stakes into the ground, but there was no way. Every stake was bending due to the hard packed gravel that obviously extended underneath this grassy spot. Also, we noticed the dumpsters we had been warned about. They were just across the street from us; the hits just kept coming. Michelle sat down and looked at our wet tent, our bent tent stakes, the stinky dumpsters across the street, I could see the expression on her face and knew she was nearing her breaking point. She pointed out another issue as she looked across the road from our site, the dump station for the entire campground was our next-door neighbor. Suddenly the dam broke, and she began weeping in her hands.

It didn't take me long to realize what happened to cause the sudden outburst. I smelt it before I saw it. A camper had pulled up to the dump station across the street and failed to connect the hose of their sewage tank properly to the dump station. When they opened the line, the hose blew off and human excrement was now spilling all over the ground.

"What a crappy situation," Michelle exclaimed crying into her hands.

"What do you want to do, quit and go home?"

"Is that an option?"

"No, that is not an option."

"Ok, leave me alone, let me cry, give me a few minutes and I will get up and we can figure this out."

I stood in the rain with bent tent stakes, an upset wife, raw sewage running down the road, and wondered aloud what I was doing in Pennsylvania. This was just a no good, very bad day. The kind that makes you second guess everything, the type of day where the building pressure of weeks on the road finally catches up to you. I took a deep breath and the thought, "don't quit on a bad day" came to mind. We say it in hiking, why can't we say it in life. After all, we were alive, healthy, and had a good day in the busy traffic of the northeast.

I returned to the park office and told them of our calamity. They agreed to move us to a better spot that they held open for such issues. Things were going to work out, a better spot, closer to the bathrooms, with water, and a tent pad. We set up, settled in, caught our breath, and knew tomorrow was going to be a better day.

Hikers deal with this on a regular basis. Days of rain, injuries, and cold wet nights can weigh on the human psyche. For the ones that finish the answers are similar when asked the question, "why didn't you quit?"

"When I wanted to quit, I remembered why I started."

"I was determined to never quit on a bad day, and I knew I wouldn't quit on a good day, so I just kept walking."

"I wanted to quit several times, but I knew my friends needed me, I couldn't go home and leave them."

"I just kept telling myself, this is your dream, you've worked too hard to quit."

These answers hold amazing nuggets of truth. Read them again. The first thing to do on a bad day is remember your "why." Why did you originally become a Pastor, why did you start the Bible study in your home, why did you plant the church, why did you begin working with students? Too often our minds drift away from our "why." I love the saying, "if you remember your why, you can go through anyhow." Remember why you started.

If you are determined to never quit on a bad day you are much less likely to give up on your dreams. But what if something needs to end? When you have thought things through with a level head, and prayerfully decided it is best to end a venture, you can now do it with no regrets.

Having a bad day is natural, feeling unfit and over-whelmed happens. One key to not quitting on a bad day is thinking about all the people who will be affected other than you. Hikers often say their friends keep them going, not wanting to leave them. We all have people who depend on us, our leadership, our example. Think about those who will be affected if we abandon our post.

Many of us have dreams. The dream is to open your own business, plant a church, launch out into a new ministry. We go through the process of seeing these things happen. Then, when trials come, on a bad day or series of days, we become tempted to pack up and head home. To go back to an easier way. We need to stop and remember when the things we have now were just dreams. Look at how far God has brought us. Remember, the God who brought you here will carry you through.

The enemy of our souls waits on the perfect time to launch his attacks on our calling and our dreams. He is a dream stealer and destroyer of all things that are good and advancing the kingdom. 1 Peter 5:8 describes the enemy as a roaring lion seeking whom he may devour. When you study lions, you find they are masters of timing. They don't rush in full attack mode when the herd is well nourished and healthy. They wait until they've worn down, sickly, in search of water, and then the lion moves in to attack. Lions wait for bad days.

We all go through ups and downs, sometimes several times within a single day. It is easy to become emotional during a string of down days, but our emotions can be terrible indicators of what is going on in our lives. It is important to never make an emotional decision in the middle of a bad day.

LESSON 9
BLOWN OFF COURSE

*And it happened that the father of Publius
lay sick of a fever and dysentery. Paul
went into him and prayed, and he laid
his hands on him and healed him.*

— ACTS 28:8 NKJV

I t was hot in the waning days of June. Shenandoah National Park was full of visitors, and we were seeing the natural beauty here for the first time. The high meadows with deer and bear. The tourists ignoring the warning signs and traipsing across the meadows to get a better look or snapping the perfect Instagram photo. The road through the park was beautiful and crowded.

Skyline drive runs 105 miles through Shenandoah National Park; it's the only public road through the park. It can be entered at four or five different locations along the scenic drive. One of the biggest attractions for travelers are the roadside pull offs and overlooks. You can see for a hundred miles across the gorgeous Shenandoah Valley below. A historic valley, home to Civil War Generals, and battles alike, but the Sassers' were there for a different reason.

The park is home to a 101 mile stretch of the Appalachian Trail. The trail zigzags across Skyline Drive many times in this distance. In the places where there is a road crossing of the Appalachian Trail, and a pull off to park, we find our best areas to set up and provide Trail Blessings for hikers.

A typical Trail Blessing will have fresh fruit, hotdogs or hamburgers, individual bags of chips and snacks, along with drinks, Gatorade, and water. The menu and setup vary depending on what is locally available, what we have on hand, and what people have blessed us with to take. On this trip we looked for the best spot to set up our Trail Blessing. The perfect spot will include cell service, a bathroom, easy drive-up access to the location, and is located next to the Appalachian Trail. This was a tall order, but we found the perfect spot.

Nestled along Skyline Drive there is a picnic area, a small loop just off the main drive. This has a series of picnic tables right beside the Appalachian Trail only steps from the truck, a bathroom, and good cell service under shade trees. An oasis in the middle of a hot summer day. We set up, had several hikers come by, and got to have communion with a group that happened to have travel communion cups. What a great day. We decided that we would be back to set up here tomorrow!

I woke early, excited to have found such a nice spot to feed hungry hikers. We packed quickly, knowing this perfect area would be gone if we waited too late; taken by a picnicking family from Wisconsin, or a bird watcher from Georgia. I rounded the corner of the loop, and to my chagrin, our spot was already taken by a well-meaning fellow handing out Gatorade. I tried to put my best face on, but I knew it was bad trail etiquette to set up too near another do-gooder. We would have to find a new spot and I wasn't happy.

"I guarantee you we will not find a better spot to set up. We'll end up somewhere with no shade, no cell service, no running water, and no bathroom."

"Well, you need to check your attitude and remember why you're out here in the first place," came Michelle's reply.

She was right, I hated it when she was right. Being reminded that I'm wrong usually does nothing to repair my moodiness on such occasions. We would end up driving fifteen miles in the opposite direction before we found another decent area to pull over and, wouldn't you know it, I was right. No shade, no bathroom, no cell service, this was great. I hated being right in these circumstances. I got our tables set up, and set out the fruit, still brooding over the aggravation of moving. The day was almost half gone.

Then, almost on cue, out of the woods came our first hiker of the day. I could tell she was young, and nearly as small as my twelve-year-old daughter. She hurried over, asked if this was trail magic, and immediately broke down in a river of tears. I was startled at the tears, not regular sniffles, I'm talking full on sobs. I took a step back and looked at my wife, I was a little unprepared for this. We got her calmed down and sat her in a camping chair. She began eating an apple and telling us about herself. Her trail name was Squirrel, she was from Germany, she had never backpacked before this trip, or left Europe. Squirrel was very homesick, her gear was wet from the daily rainstorms that plague the trail in summertime, and she hadn't had cell service to call her family or boyfriend in several days. She was on the verge of quitting the hike and heading home defeated.

"I was just so happy to see a family," she explained as her reason for the outburst of tears. "I'm so glad you guys were here; I feel like you were here just for me." That's when it hit me, we were here just for her. We had our whole day rearranged, our comfortable spot under the shade tree, our nice bathroom, all changed because God knew there was a young lady from Germany that was broken and hurting. Someone who needed the love of Christ on a very rough day.

I explained to her that we weren't supposed to be in this area. We had another place picked, but through a series of circumstances, God brought us here. Yes, he brought me here in spite of all my best efforts, and even though I was aggravated by the circumstances. He had us here just for her. We shared God's love with her, prayed with her, visited for a time, and she headed northbound on the Appalachian Trail. We had friends who hiked with her in Connecticut, and she continued north, finishing the trail.

When I think about this story and being blown off course; things not going my way, but being perfectly in God's plan, I see parallels to the Apostle Paul when he was being taken to Rome. He was a prisoner put into the care of a centurion, He gave good advice, but the majority overruled him and chose to sail on into the winter storms, he ended up in two weeks of punishing storms, then was shipwrecked in the freezing waters of the Adriatic Sea. To top it off, when he finally washed ashore on a broken piece of wood, he was bitten on the hand by a poisonous snake while gathering firewood. What a time he was having. But there is a bigger picture.

The chief of the island, Publius, had a sick father. They brought Paul who prayed for him, and the father was healed. Then they brought others afflicted with sicknesses to Paul and they were also healed. Is it possible that Paul was blown one hundred eighty-six miles off course, went through storms, a shipwreck, and was bitten by a snake, all because there was a sick man, and people on the island, who needed a touch from God?

Too often we envision a life free of storms, free of bad days, with no compounding hardships. That simply isn't a realistic picture of life. However, we need to remember that occasionally there is a reason we've been blown off course. So, things aren't going your way? I've learned to step back and ask God if there is a reason that I'm in a particular place. Maybe we must visit the doctor more often than we like, is there someone sitting next to us in that doctor's office that needs a smile, a kind word. Perhaps, you're running late, stuck in the bleachers at a ballgame, have to make an extra trip to the store for something you forgot, or aggravated at the place life has taken you, remember, you may be in the very place God would have you be to minister to a specific person.

LESSON 10
LETTING GO OF DEAD THINGS

*Forget the former things; do not dwell on the
past. See, I am doing a new thing! Now it
springs up; do you not perceive it? I am
making a way in the desert and streams
in the wasteland.*

— ISAIAH 43: 18-19 NIV

In Alabama one of the surest signs of winter is colder
days; in East Tennessee there is another sight that
ushers in winter, the colors of autumn. I remember
staring up the mountains at the beautiful hues of red,
orange, and yellow, interspersed with several shades of
green. I'd read about this, seen pictures in books, but
now I laid eyes upon the colored mountains surrounding
country chapels, old red barns, and pumpkin patches.
Even though I now called these mountains home, I
became a tourist for a few moments. It's easy to get lost

in the kaleidoscope of colors that late fall brings to the hills.

These trees, with their array of colors, provide a needed resource in Appalachia. A resource that many small towns in the area depend heavily upon, tourism. Jobs in these communities can be hard to come by for many native Appalachians, the hospitality and service industry, catering to out of towners, is a main employer. In Damascus, the Appalachian Trail, the Virginia Creeper Trail, trout fishing, and motorcycle tourism keep this small town afloat. One outfitter who does bike rentals for the Virginia Creeper told me they have every time slot full for the month of October. Sometimes these slots are all taken by early June, tourists wanting to ride through the colors of fall. Everyone knows they have a small window to see this phenomenon, and then the trees will release these dying leaves to the ground.

In this natural occurrence we see the new growth of spring, turn into the beauty of fall, and then move into the depths of winter, only to prepare for new growth again. The key is, unless the tree lets the dead leaves fall, no matter how beautiful they were, there can't be new growth. Sometimes we must let the dead things of the past go.

Each of us have things in our lives that have required release, or they burden us forever. There are dead relationships, business opportunities, family squabbles, friendships, the list goes on. Just as the trees must release their leaves, no matter how beautiful they once were, we must release the dead things of our past so we can grow into the beauty of our future.

One key here is forgiveness. The Bible speaks about forgiveness over and over. Jesus talks about forgiveness, the Old and New Testaments both mention it. Forgiveness is paramount in our quest to be free from the past. Whatever the perceived wrong might be, when we can extend forgiveness, we no longer have to carry that burden. It's amazing how freedom comes from forgiveness. When we fail to forgive, we fail to release the past from our grasp. If we want to move forward, leaving that past hurt behind, we must forgive.

In Philippians chapter 3, Paul states, "forgetting those things which are behind, reaching towards the things which are before, I press towards the mark." Sometimes the hardest person to forgive is yourself. Satan is an accuser and will constantly bring up old things, dead things. He will remind you of past failures, until we realize that if we are in Christ there is no more condemnation for the past. God has forgiven you, and you must let it go. There is nothing that can be done about the past, but everything can become beautiful in the future.

Paul was an accuser, and a murderer of believers. He had a lot of past remorse, I'm sure. No doubt he met people as he traveled who could have been family members of Christians he helped send to their doom. He knew the importance of letting go of dead things and pressing towards the future.

Part of my testimony are the family issues that

presented themselves early in my life. Mistakes made that affected my life, not of my own doing. As I have grown older, I've had choices to make regarding these, somewhat traumatic, experiences of my early childhood. Would I hold onto old grudges, would I blame everyone else for the mistakes I've made, blame my childhood trauma, or would I extend forgiveness. Could I extend forgiveness, let go of dead things, and see the beautiful new growth that had sprung forth. I chose the latter and that has made a huge difference in my life.

E.M. Blaiklock gives us a great example of what can come from letting go. He tells that when the French recovered the battered shell of the Rheims Cathedral, they performed a restoration of every stone and statue. This was painstaking, time consuming, a last gasp to hold onto a relic. However, when the Athenians found the Hekatompedon burnt down, they let it lie, found a new site, and built the Parthenon.

Holding onto the past will not make you better, it will only make you bitter. Imagine those trees holding onto those leaves after the color has gone. Past the natural point of release. Trees filled with dead, crumpled, withered leaves. The dull shade of brown that would cover the hillside. That's what our lives are like when we can't forgive the hurts and release the past. The new won't come if the old leaf remains. Don't dwell on the past, prepare for the beauty of the future.

LESSON 11
THE PROVISION OF GOD

I have been young, and now I'm old; Yet I
have not seen the righteous forsaken, Nor
his seed begging bread.

— PSALMS 37:25 NKJV

Any missionary who has been in the field, no
doubt, has many stories of the Lord's provision.
Especially financial provision. I will give my disclaimer, I
do not feel everyone who loves the Lord will get rich, far
from it. If financial prosperity was the endgame for the
Christian life, then someone has a lot of explaining to do
regarding the prophets and apostles of the Bible. I am
not against money; the kingdom advances because good
people, who have been blessed financially, give of their
abundance cheerfully. I pray that you are all blessed.
Okay, now here's my story.

Once again, we found ourselves at Pine Grove

Furnace State Park. This park serves as the midpoint of the Appalachian Trail, has a huge campground filled with hikers, and a booming general store. For these reasons and more, you can find the Sassers' here on a yearly basis. This was the summer of 2020, just after things began to reopen after the pandemic.

We decided to grab some drinks and hike northbound on the Appalachian Trail, it was July 1st and very hot. We knew the ten miles just before Pine Grove Furnace had been in a prescribed burn, and shade was hard to come by. We could hand out drinks to the hikers we passed, make an introduction, and invite them to come back to our campsite that night and have dinner with us. It wasn't long before we found some hikers enjoying a stream with a wooden bridge crossing above. We passed out the drinks, a few stickers, and found that our new friends were already planning to camp at the park. They would be in the site opposite us. Neighbors! Even better, one hiker was accompanied by his daughter who enjoyed hiking. The kids were happy to have someone to play with back at camp.

That evening, after a visit to the swimming hole, we started the fire and roasted corn. One of the best things about Pennsylvania is the corn. In my mind I see Pennsylvania as a big cornfield. We always try to find a local fruit and vegetable stand, sometimes we visit the Amish stands nearby, and get food for hikers. Roasted corn over the fire is a treat for weary hikers who can't carry fruits and veggies in their packs. It was a good evening, after we ate the adults talked and the kids played. It was a peaceful summer evening, just about golden hour, everything was good in the world, and then it wasn't.

I have learned to appreciate good times because life can turn on a dime. You never know what will come down the pipe in this fallen creation. What happened next was without a doubt the scariest moment of my life. Remember, in a previous story I mentioned the second scariest moment, this was the first. I think it was even worse because it involved one of the kids.

Lane, at the time thirteen years old, the day before his fourteenth birthday, was riding a razor scooter in a parking lot only 30 feet from our campsite. The other kids were throwing a frisbee back and forth across the lot. As Lane came by, he reached up with one hand to catch the frisbee, while holding onto the scooter with the other. This spun him around and threw him violently to the ground, the back of his heading hitting the pavement with a loud crack. I jumped up and was next to him in a flash. His eyes were fixed, motionless, but open. His chest heaved up and down in an unnatural breathing, but there seemed to be a struggle. Everything around me seemed to be in slow motion. Due to the remoteness of this area people struggled with cell service to call 9-11. One of our new friends ran to a landline phone, the other joined me next to Lane, and my wife ran down the road trying to find a nurse. Lane's chest stopped moving up and down. "Lane" "Lane" I was inches from his face screaming his name, trying to get him to come around. I leaned down and blew into his mouth. I'd been CPR certified many years before, but never had to use any of the training. Suddenly, Lane's eyes snapped open, he took a huge breath, tears rolled down his cheeks, and he mumbled, "what happened?"

It was apparent from the first few moments that Lane had a concussion. A nurse came running from a few campsites down to provide some aid. It didn't take long for the ambulance to arrive and whisk Lane away to the hospital, the first of two hospitals we would be admitted to. The first hospital said he had a small skull fracture and a major concussion, but they didn't have a pediatric neuro doctor. So, Lane would have to travel by ambulance to Hershey, Pennsylvania, where they had the proper doctors to care for a teenager.

A quick aside. We love the town of Hershey. The story of Mr. and Mrs. Hershey is fascinating. Apparently, they couldn't have children and endowed various children's homes, local schools, and a hospital, which happened to have some of the best children's trauma doctors in the country. The hospital we were transferred to in Hershey, PA, was top-notch.

We spent the next three days in Hershey, PA. It was July 2nd- 5th, to be exact. I remember looking out the big windows on the upper floors and watching the fireworks shooting off at Hershey Park. The long stay was due to Lane not holding down food. All head injuries are different; this one hit the area of the brain, which monitored motion sickness causing Lane to constantly feel nauseous. When we were finally released, it took us several days to get home because Lane could only ride a few hours at a time.

We were so thankful to all the people that reached out in prayer. Also, some helped us financially along the way, paying for hotel stays and sending love offerings to help us get home. It was indeed a blessing. Finally, we settled in at home to await the inevitable; what would the medical bills look like when they arrived?

Those first few bills came in, and they weren't too bad. Maybe we were going to be ok from this hospital stay after all. No matter what, we trusted the Lord and his provision. Finally, we had three bills arrive from ambulance companies, and that was when we took the hit. We learned that ambulance companies are rarely in network with any insurance companies. Our total ambulance bills for the original transport, and the additional moves, totaled nearly five thousand dollars.

The ambulance bill was shocking, but honestly, we were overwhelmed by God's goodness and that Lane seemed to be okay. We knew the Lord had not brought us to this place to leave us and he would make a way. We prayed, trusted the Lord, and began to make plans for paying the ambulance bills. That's when God showed up.

Several years earlier, when Lane was a baby, I filled in for a precious congregation in South Alabama. These were salt of the earth people, down home folks, the kind you don't mind driving two and a half hours one way to preach for every weekend. Honestly, looking back, I think it was more zeal and excitement for ministry, and youthful exuberance. I'm not sure forty-year-old Brad could handle it, but I digress. We loved these folks and our time there.

When the current Pastor called to tell me, the congregation wanted to help us with medical bills I was surprised. We didn't speak about amounts or bills, he just mentioned they had taken up an offering and it was on the way. I was blown away when the check came; a check that paid off the ambulance bills within two dollars. If I said I didn't sit down and cry I'd be a liar. The provision of God is a real deal. You can count on it. Truly, I have never seen the righteous forsaken.

I want to add one more nugget. When the check came in, God reminded me of a Sunday morning at this little church that I had forgotten. While we were filling in, we had a Gideon speaker come one Sunday morning. I remember clearly the Lord impressing upon me to give my salary from that Sunday to the Gideon offering. That was a big reach for a young family, but I knew it was the Lord, and gladly gave it. I know Luke 6:38 has been misused by some, but the Lord let me know this was a prime example. The verse states, "Give, and it will be given to you. A good measure, pressed down, shaken together and running over, will be poured into your lap. For with the measure you use, it will be measured to you." (Luke 6:38 NIV)

LESSON 12
RENEWED STRENGTH

But those who wait on the LORD shall renew
their strength; They shall mount up with
wings like eagles, They shall run and not
be weary, They shall walk and not faint.

— ISAIAH 40:31 NKJV

Thru Hikers -yes, I know this is a misspelling, but it's how we write it on the trail- will tell you each year of a unique phenomenon. Every year you hear hikers in Pennsylvania, or some other northern state, say something like, "Georgia was tough, but I thought Virginia was flat and easy, really everything above Virginia has been easy." This helps propagate the myth that Virginia is flat and easy, which is not the case at all. If it's not the case, then why do so many thru hikers seem to think this? The answer is simple, the trail didn't get easier, they simply got stronger.

Every difficult step in Georgia prepares you for the later steps you will take. All the days going straight up in the Great Smoky Mountains are training for the hike through the Shenandoahs. In reality, nothing has gotten easier. The days are still long, the hills are still tough to climb, and it's still backpacking, but the difficult first weeks have turned you into a well-oiled machine. One whose legs can churn out mile after mile, someone who doesn't blink at mileage that once, several months back, would have been impossible.

The journey is still the same, but hikers are physically more capable of the journey. They have gotten stronger, their strength renewed, growing day over day. For me it isn't a stretch to see the comparisons with life.

In 2 Corinthians 12:7, Paul, writing to the church in Corinth, mentions a "thorn in the flesh." We aren't told exactly what Paul was dealing with. Some believe this was a reference to a person who caused trouble for him, other theories include migraines, chronic eye problems, or seizures. Some believe he was speaking in metaphors, and this wasn't an actual physical affliction. Whatever the issue, we know Paul was dealing with a problem, and asked the Lord to remove it from him, yet it stayed with him. Do I believe God hears our prayers? Absolutely I do! Do I believe that God is a healer of the broken? Yes, without question. However, I also know God is sovereign, he cannot be manipulated, nor bent to our will and command.

There are times in my life that the Lord has healed me from disease and affliction. Then, there are things that he has given me the grace to carry. Much the way Paul was stricken yet said, "Nonetheless your grace is sufficient for me." There are times when God removes the burden, and times when he gives us the renewed strength to carry the weight. Do we wish that life was easy? Absolutely, we would all love easy, carefree, stress-less lives, but we're never promised that. We are promised just the opposite.

Jesus says, "In the world you will have tribulation, but be of good cheer, I have overcome the world." (John 16:33 NKJV) God never said the Christian life was going to be easy, he just said it was going to be worth it. Remember our earlier lesson on the lighter pack? When the load is more than we can handle, the Lord helps us carry the weight. He walks with us in the hills and valleys of life, never leaving or forsaking us. We are over-comers because he was an overcomer.

Often the strength we glean from the journey is not automatic. In hiking, hikers talk about getting their trail legs. This is the process, often weeks long, of training your muscles to respond to the constant barrage of daily miles. It can be a long, painful process that ultimately makes them extremely efficient. Likewise, when we are walking the tuff miles of life, we gain confidence in the Lord, our faith increases, he strengthens us day by day, but it can take time.

Isaiah clearly states, "those who wait." Our modern, American way of life is one that is not conducive to waiting. We want instant fixes, fast food, shots that instantly deaden the pain. We read the cliff notes, watch the movie rather than read the book, and depend on the GPS to give us the fastest point from A to B. We don't have patience, or time, to take the scenic route, or stop and smell the roses. I think God smiles at us when he allows us to wait. Teaching us that our timelines are small things compared to his master plan. Ultimately in this process God strengthens us and sustains us.

LESSON 13
GOD OF MIRACLES

*Jesus looked at them and said, "With man
this is impossible, but with God all things
are possible."*

— MATTHEW 19:26 NKJV

Albert Einstein once said, "there are two ways to live your life. One is as though nothing is a miracle. The other is as though everything is a miracle." I tend to agree with this, and I chose to live as though everything is a miracle. The mere fact that you and I are standing on a rock moving around the Sun at 67,000 miles per hour, while at the same time the Earth spins at 1,000 miles per hour, yet we aren't obliterated due to natural laws; this is a miracle to me. Miracles are all around us, we just need to open our eyes.

"I want to tell you about a miracle, Chaplain." At least I think it's a miracle, I'll let you decide."

When a story starts with these words, I take immediate notice. "Okay, let me hear it."

He went on to tell me the story of a young lady who was severely burned while hiking. She had hiked hard that morning and decided to stop for lunch. She, like most hikers, had a small stove with a cookpot that sits atop. Usually hikers pour water, and whatever concoction they wish to cook, into the pot and let it boil. The best practice is to sit the stove on a flat surface; a picnic table, or the floor of a shelter will do the trick. That day she decided to take a shortcut, a costly shortcut. She sat the boiling pot on her legs in her lap. The pot overturned and she had a large spot on her upper leg that was badly burned. What could she do? She realized there was only one thing she could do, she had to hike. Being 12-15 miles from the closet town, and having no medical supplies, she began to hobble towards help. As she walked the pain intensified, she was worried about the possibilities of infection. A very real worry in the wilderness. There was one shelter before town, she decided to make it there and rest for a few minutes, then hike hard into town. Now limping, the young lady prayed silently to herself, she asked the Lord to help her make it to town, to please not let the wound become infected, and please ease the pain.

As she approached the shelter she saw, to her dismay, nobody was around. She had hoped to encounter others, perhaps someone with a medical kit, or another hiker who could give her advice. The shelter was a ghost town. She sat down, removed her pack, and put her head in her hands for a good cry, that's when something caught her eye. This shelter, like some others, had a picnic table sitting near it. She walked over and what she found floored her. There, on the picnic table, in the middle of nowhere, with no other person around, she found gauze, burn cream, antiseptic spray, the works. She said it was all in pristine condition, it didn't look like it had been walking around in some other hiker's backpack. It looked like it had been placed there just for her. Our friend was able to treat the wound, get some relief from the pain, and get into town to see the doctor.

"So, you think that was a miracle?"

My response was, "yes, I think that's a miracle."

In my seventeen years of ministry, I have seen God do impossible things. In fact, Jesus says it two ways in the Bible. He says nothing is impossible, and all things are possible to those who believe.

It seems we often over complicate the business of prayer and the miraculous. Our friend who burned her leg didn't adhere to the traditional three Ls of miraculous prayer. I say this jokingly, but it is true. The three Ls are: long, loud, and low. If you want to see God move on your behalf you must pray a long prayer, it must be loud and boisterous, and you might have to get low and lay on the ground. However, this young lady prayed a very simple, very humble, childlike prayer.

In 1 Kings 18 we see this principle in the story of Elijah and the prophets of Baal. When it was Elijah's turn to call down fire from heaven, he uttered a simple prayer. A prayer of less than 100 words was the catalyst that brought down fire from heaven. I have nothing against the three L's. Long, low, and loud has its place, but I've seen God move just the same from a simple, "Do it Lord Jesus, receive your glory Lord."

Belief is our job, the miraculous is God's job. We must be careful that we don't get too caught up thinking we can do God's job. Often, I have found that the prayers I've prayed and forgotten about have seen miraculous results. I'm literally more shocked than anyone when God answers in the affirmative because I had given it to the Lord and let it be. In those cases, I spent no energy trying to do God's job for him. Abraham and Sara had to learn this lesson the hard way. In Genesis 17 they were promised to become the parents of nations. Then after a while they decided it was time to "help" God out. Obviously, they weren't having children at their age, so Abraham would have to use Hagar to accomplish God's purpose. Of course, this was a huge problem, one with implications for future generations, and a great lesson to us. Belief is our job, the miraculous is God's job. Let God handle it.

I know some listen to the story of the hiker finding the bandages and immediately think of all the reasons the supplies were there. Another hiker must have left them. Someone forgot to put them back in their bag, or the items were taking up space, so they were discarded. One thing to remember is there will always be naysayers. If I had a nickel for every naysaying Nancy or complaining Carl I've encountered, I'd be rich. No offense if your name is Nancy or Carl. Someone will always have an issue or explanation, but I remind them that even if the items were discarded, they still answered a desperate prayer. Think of the set of circumstances that must happen for those items to be left by a hiker.

Someone had to buy those items before their hike, thinking it's likely they will need them. Then, at the exact point our friend would come along needing the supplies, they had to decide they would not need them, and leave them on a picnic table. The trail is 2200 miles, give or take. What are the chances? Perhaps it's not impossible but it is improbable. I personally tend to not believe in coincidences. So many times, we say, "Wow, what a coincidence." When we should be saying, "Wow, what a God." Because the things naysayers call weird coincidences, strange happenings, questionable timing, that's just God working.

Another point I've found to be true about miracles is this, miracles tend to happen at the edges. Let me illustrate this point with a story from a missionary. It was said that a church in a foreign, rural, secluded mission field had heard about juice from grapes. They knew stories of Jesus turning water into wine, but never saw it. One Sunday as they prepared drawn water for communion, a parishioner asked if it were possible for them to have juice. Maybe they could pray over the water and see it transformed in wine. The missionary was surprised but agreed they could do that. Miraculously the water turned into wine. The missionary took the moment in, knowing God can do the miraculous, and seeing it done, are too different things. Those moments are still amazing, even if you believe it can be done. The congregation gave thanks and took communion. When the missionary shared the story back home in the states he was met with suspicious glares. One stateside congregant questioned him after the service, "if that was possible why haven't we seen that here in our church?" The missionary smiled, "because you can drive half a mile to the grocery store and buy all you need."

Miracles happen when you're out of options; when the only one who could possibly rectify the need is God. That's why I love hard situations, but that's where God shows up. This helps answer the question I have heard before. Why do missionaries have so many stories of miracles? Perhaps it's because they are operating at the edge, in the places of great need.

I love the story of the miraculous bandages in the wilderness of Appalachia for another reason. It's because God gets all the glory. One important factor in the miraculous is making sure God gets the glory. We must be sure God gets the glory! I love stories of the South African Evangelist William Duma. It is told that Reverend Duma would always pray, "take your Glory Lord, have your glory Lord," as God moved to heal infirmities, release the oppressed, and in a few cases, raise the dead.[1] Today, if a miracle happens at a church, people flock to that church, they want to hear that minister, they want to pray at that same altar. Now the minister at that church will get to sell thousands of books and appear on the 700 Club. Sometimes it appears everyone gets the glory except the one who is worthy of the glory. For our young hiker it was just God. No superstar preacher laid hands on her burns, she wasn't attending the right church on the right day, she said a simple, humble prayer and saw God move.

I have nothing against selling books or being interviewed on television shows. I just don't want us to lose focus. God's power isn't tied to a particular church, denomination, or seminary degree. So many miraculous things happen every day; we overlook so much. Perhaps you need God to move in a mighty way, like the hiker in our story. I'm going to pray in advance that anyone who reads this and says a simple, humble prayer will see God move mighty and miraculous on your behalf.

LESSON 14
THE NEED FOR RESUPPLY

And when they prayed, the place where they
were assembled together was shaken; and
they were all filled with the Holy Spirit,
and they spoke the word of God with
boldness.

— ACTS 4:31 NKJV

As hikers travel along the Appalachian Trail, they typically need to resupply every 3-5 days. It's a simple concept, if you fail to resupply then you run out of needed items for survival. Considering a hiker could burn four to six thousand calories on an average day hiking in Appalachia, failing to resupply could be disastrous. Every hiker likely has a story of getting close to the end of their food and water. From firsthand experience I can confirm that this brings a great deal of anxiety.

Resupplies consist of food, water, fuel for stoves, and

other miscellaneous items. Food can be a heavy item and hikers won't carry more than a few days' worth at a time. No matter the item, the need to get more of the needed supplies every few days is of utmost importance. Along the 2200-mile trail there are hundreds of locations where hikers can resupply. Many trail towns have hostels, Wal Marts, Dollar Generals, and trail angels who keep them supplied. Water is found in these locations, but more often water comes from natural sources.

The threat of dehydration, even in cooler months, should never be ignored. The rule of threes is always important to remember. Generally, you can go three minutes without oxygen, three days without water, and 30 days without food. This is approximate, and changes due to various situations, but you see the premise. You can't go far without water, and the three days are under the best conditions. Walking in the mountains will put greater strain on your body and water will need to be replenished quicker.

Blake and I were still within the first sixty miles of trail when I learned the lesson of resupplying water. We approached Hawk Mountain Shelter and the place was packed with hikers. It was near noon, and many had yet to get moving from the night before. Early on in Georgia these areas can house many hikers, it looked like a small village encamped around the shelter. I knew there was water available, but I didn't want to carry the extra weight at the time. Our map showed us the next reliable water source was near eight miles away, but we had seen a couple unmarked areas flowing already the previous two days. I was confident I wouldn't have to make it that far. I was wrong. I have since learned the trick is to go to the water source and drink all you can, even if you don't fill the bottles you carry. That way your body is hydrated, and you have added no extra external weight.

As we struggled along we decided to set up camp about six miles down trail, still no water. It was early in the evening when I ran out, but I was confident I wouldn't need it until later tomorrow. We would go hiking early while it was still cool in the morning. The next morning started with one of those unnamed, tortuous mountains. The type that goes straight up, then when it seems you've reached the top, they turn and continue upward. Yep, and her I was hiking straight up a mountain with no water. I knew I was about spent as we hiked down the mountain, but that's when help showed up in the form of the United States military.

The Army Rangers mountain phase is conducted in the North Georgia mountains. Usually these maneuvers occur out of Camp Merrill near Dahlonega, Georgia. Hikers are told to be aware that they could see these men with green faces occasionally near the trail. The Rangers carry on with their business, normally no words are exchanged if you happen to see these young soldiers with packs twice the size of our hiking packs. Often, the Rangers aren't seen at all, one only knows they've been there due to large equipment, like the water buffalo.

A "water buffalo" is used by the military to carry clean, potable water into the field where no water may be available. This is a water tank that looks like a huge drum, welded to a frame, that can be pulled behind a jeep or other military vehicle. It was a water buffalo, that had been left in the gap off the forest service road, that provided me with my water resupply. At first I wasn't sure what I was looking at, then I saw the spout, and in desperation figured it out. Blake wondered aloud if it was ok for us to use. I mentioned that it was parked in a public space, and left unlocked. Obviously, they didn't care if a couple weary hikers came by and got water. Also, if I fell out from dehydration, they would most likely be the ones called to come pluck me off the mountain. I'd heard stories of rescues turning into training exercises in these parts. I was very appreciative of the unlocked "water buffalo."

The same principle of resupply can be applied to the Christian walk. It is false to assume you can make a decision for Christ and ride out the rest of your days, needing nothing else from God. We need God daily. I need a fresh touch, must regularly read the Word of God, and require time in prayer. I love journaling my thoughts and meditating on scripture. All these practices serve as a "resupply" of sorts. They are refreshing, rejuvenating, and encouraging to those who know the Lord, or are seeking to know more.

In Psalms 61:3 the writer says, "my soul thirsts for you." The reason for this soul thirst is the same as natural thirst- it's a lack of nourishment. In this case spiritual nourishment. In the natural sense I never knew how much I really needed water to survive until I hit the spot on a trail that was dry and barren. Likewise, we will experience dry, barren places in our lives, places where nothing will satisfy the longing of our soul, but God.

The early church experienced the need for resupply, the need to satisfy the thirst of the soul. In Acts chapter 3 we see the formation of the community of believers. Immediately following were the arrests and first persecutions. Peter and John were arrested, brought before leaders, and testified with boldness of Jesus. They were threatened and told they should no longer teach these things. I would agree that's a rough day. They thought Jesus was dead, then met the resurrected Christ, were filled with the Spirit, testified with boldness, were arrested and persecuted. Yep, that is a draining sequence filled with the highest highs and lowest lows. After the stint in jail, they went to a prayer meeting and the Holy Spirit filled the place anew. They were drained, their souls were thirsty, they needed a fresh touch, and God showed up.

I wish we could feel the same excitement to wake up, pray, read the word, and worship as I felt coming down the hill toward the water buffalo. At the bottom of the hill was what I needed to survive, go on, to make it to the end of my journey. Our spiritual journeys are no different. God has the nourishment you need at the ready, prepared to resupply you, and bless you on the journey ahead.

LESSON 15
THE FEW WHO FINISH

For Demas has forsaken me, having loved this present world, and has departed for Thessalonica

— 2 TIMOTHY 4:10 NKJV

Every year thousands of hikers make plans to hike the complete twenty-two hundred miles of the Appalachian Trail. These are not halfhearted plans in most cases, these are individuals who have taken extreme steps. They've quit jobs, or gone on sabbatical, they've spent hundreds, in many cases thousands of dollars on equipment, subleased apartments and sold houses all for the chance to hike the Trail. Even with this level of preparation, less than 25% of those who begin the trail will stand atop Mt. Katahdin in Maine. We've already covered the various issues that hikers deal with on trail. They range from constant rain, and twisted ankles to depression, anxiety, and burnout. Whatever the reason, the attrition rate for the journey is high.

Hikers will tell you losing a beloved hiking partner, or trail family member is a huge downer. There is an emptiness that is felt as they walk out of town knowing it may be months, or years, before they see their friends again. In some cases, hikers chose to leave the trail and go home themselves after a beloved hiking partner leaves. They will say it just isn't the same, the experience has changed. For some the feeling of abandonment is overwhelming. Particularly if the hiking partner was a friend from back home, now their last piece of home has left them, and they are more homesick than ever. These are just a few of the myriad of reasons for leaving the trail.

It is easy for me to see parallels in the Christian walk and the journey of hikers on the trail. As a more seasoned Christian I can look back eighteen years or so and remember all the dear friends who started on a journey very similar to mine. They had callings, anointing, and several were probably better looking. I jest, but truthfully these were very talented people being used by the Lord in amazing ways. As I survey the landscape nearly twenty years later there are many, who started with so much promise, that are no longer in ministry, some who flat out don't live for the Lord at all. This is one of the saddest things to see. To see someone with the call, the ability, the desire, sitting behind a desk at a used car dealership, running a multi-level marketing scheme, or running a successful business that has nothing to do with service of the kingdom. We must know to succeed at anything other than what God has called us to do is to fail. It doesn't matter how much money you have, how much you give, how much you volunteer, or how much good you do. If you are not following the will of God for your life you are failing.

Unfortunately, it's not just those who are called to ministry that I've shed tears over. In my years of ministry, I have become fond of, loved, several people who have been in my congregations. As a youth pastor you pour all you can into young people, trying to steer them in the proper direction. You see them saved, baptized, filled with the love of the Lord, and in some cases they walk away. To see those, you love making decisions detrimental to the rest of their lives knowing there is nothing you can do to stop it, is a horrible feeling. I've lived both sides of this and it's a traumatic, sad road either way.

The Apostle Paul knew this all too well. Over the course of ministry, he had seen many sons and daughters in the faith raised up. He too, had seen many who once walked faithfully with him fall by the wayside. He knew the pain of seeing his associates fall away and stop following the Lord. In the case of Demas, Paul states he left for Thessalonica. Thessalonica means false victory. When people turn their backs on callings, and anointings, for money, houses, and things, they are leaving the Lord for a false victory. It may look good for a season, but there is no hope in this victory.

Like Demas, many chose to forgo their faith because

they "have loved this present world." The draw of the world, selfishness, swayed them from the purpose of God in their lives. John Greenleaf Whittier once said, "Of all sad words of tongue or pen, the saddest are these 'It might have been." What might have been? What might your life have been, if only you'd chosen to live in full devotion to the Lord. What might have been?

This question rings loud when analyzing the life of Charles Templeton. Templeton was a contemporary of Billy Graham. He and Billy roomed together as they ministered in Europe and became good friends during this time. In the 40s and 50s he was a leading evangelist, some have said he had more talent, and was better looking, than his counterpart Billy Graham. So why did Billy Graham become a household name, perhaps the greatest preacher of his generation, while the name Charles Templeton has been lost to history? The answer is surprisingly simple, Billy Graham walked faithfully according to the calling on his life and was elevated in a way that only comes from God opening the doors. While Templeton began to doubt God, moving forward in his intellectual pursuits he became an agnostic, and finally progressed to atheism. Templeton wrote a book, *Farewell to God*, where he outlined problematic questions concerning the Bible narratives. Truly, Templeton's story is a sad illustration of a life that echoes, "What might have been."[1]

For sure nobody wakes up one day and decides to become an apostate. It's not a spontaneous decision. It's failure that creeps in little by little. A few trips to the lake, or the golf course, rather than taking the family to church. Nights with friends that get later and later, partying harder, and feeling fewer tugs of the Holy Spirit upon your heart. It's the slow fade; moving from inconsistency to compromise, and finally to a complete falling away.

If inconsistency is the cause, consistency is the cure. Developing consistent routines with our personal Bible study and prayer. Consistent fellowship with a local body of believers. Surrounding ourselves with others who have a consistent walk with the Lord. It's not perfection, but the daily attempt to become more Christ-like. These consistent habits will allow us to navigate the highs and lows, ebbs, and flows, of life victoriously.

For each of us the goal of our Christian walk should be to say as the Apostle Paul in 2 Timothy 4:7, "I have fought a good fight, I have finished my course, I have kept the faith." (KJV) To be faithful to the end is the goal. It doesn't say to be perfect to the end, but to fight and be faithful. You have to realize that your faith is worth fighting for, your family is worth fighting for, your calling is worth fighting for, your destiny is worth fighting for. If we're still contending for the faith, still fighting to be more like Christ, we're going to make it to the end of the journey. We're going to hear well done.

LESSON 16
POWER

But you shall receive power when the Holy
Spirit has come upon you, and you shall
be witnesses to Me in Jerusalem, and in
all Judea and Samaria, and to the end of
the earth.

— ACTS 1:8 NKJV

We recently purchased a small lot in Shady Valley, TN. Shady Valley is a beautiful high valley located between the NASCAR town of Bristol, TN and the college town of Boone, NC. The best thing is it's within four miles of two road crossings of the Appalachian Trail which provides perfect access to hikers.

There was no water or power on the lot at first. We survived like this for several months before calling in reinforcements. My brother Derek and his family came up with us to help me work on the water and power. The concrete slab on the lot allows us to set up our campers together around the slab, creating our own little community between the RVs. Due to not having power we set up hanging lanterns, had a fire going, and made sure the kids had plenty of flashlights. The importance of light is due more to numerous potholes than Black Bears who frequent the area.

One night while returning from a walk after sunset, Derek mentioned how the lot was lit up so bright you'd think we had power. I remember agreeing, the area around the camper is wild, there is eleven miles of Cherokee National Forest land running behind our lot, the lights from the lanterns contrasted brightly against the dark backdrop of lightless mountains. Derek commented that driving past it looked like we had power. "You'd never guess from looking at that setup that we don't actually have power." It was this comment that got me thinking, you know, we Christians are a lot like the trailers parked on the lot. Often, we look the part, we seem like we are walking in the power and authority of God, but it's just fake light. We fail to walk in power because we don't understand it, or our character can't handle it.

The biggest cause of powerlessness is lack of understanding. Know this, you are powerless, outside of Christ. Ephesians 6:10 says, "Finally, my brethren, be strong in the Lord and in the POWER of his might." We put confidence in everything we can see, when Christ, who we can't see, promises he will never leave us. The

Holy Spirit dwells within the believer. Now, imagine Jesus himself walking up to us, dressed in white robes with a purple sash, looking just like the picture on your Great Grandmother's wall. Feathered hair flowing, reminding you of Barry Gibb from the Bee Gees in the 70s. In that moment you would believe anything was possible, you have Jesus with you, power personified is walking with you. My confidence in God's power would be overwhelming. Why do we not have the same confidence knowing the Holy Spirit is with us? If I sent you to the store with two dollars to buy a coke, you would get a coke. What if I sent you with eight quarters? You could still buy the same thing; you would still have two dollars just in a different form. The Holy Spirit who resides in you gives you the same purchasing power as Jesus himself walking with you.

Imagine if we had our power hooked up but continued to use the little lanterns to light our campers. That's the way many Christians operate. They are hooked to the source but fail to properly allow the power to flow. We need to turn the power on, put ourselves out there, pray for people, allow God room to move. Many times, people ask us to pray, and our response is, "sure I will." We tell them we'll be praying for them, then we halfheartedly remember the need late at night during our bedtime prayers. Why not pray for them on the spot? Right there on the sidewalk, in the middle of the office, or at Walmart. We don't pray because we lack confidence, we're uncomfortable, because we're hooked up to the source, but we don't allow the power to flow. This happens in churches. A member has a request, an urgent need, desperate for someone to touch heaven on their behalf. The pastor, preacher, priest, or whatever title we give to the one in charge mentions the need, makes a note, and moves on with the service. After all, there is an order, a schedule to be kept. I ask the age-old question, what would Jesus do? I believe he'd stop everything; he'd call the saints of God to prayer on the spot, he'd lay hands on the sick with confidence that they would be healed. Let's not forget this is biblical. James 5:14-16 says, "Is anyone among you sick? Let him call for the elders of the church, and let them pray over him, anointing him with oil in the name of the Lord." Activate your faith, let God be God, power is God's part, believing him for it is my part.

God will never place a greater anointing upon you than your character can bear. We know that pride was a primary cause of Satan's fall. For some pride and ego are barriers to the power of God working in their lives. If they could walk in great anointing, they might allow themselves to be exalted rather than God. Humility and anointing, the power of God go hand in hand. The Bible is filled with individuals who had the humblest of beginnings.

Moses was a slave, Saul was from the smallest tribe, David was the youngest son, Nehemiah was a cupbearer, Ezekiel was in slavery, Peter and John were fishermen from Galilee, the list goes on. Each of them anointed, used by God; the only one listed here who failed was

Saul, and his failure was losing humility and falling into selfishness and sinfulness. Character counts with God.

Another story comes to mind when discussing power. Anyone who spends time driving in the mountains will attest to the wear and tear on a vehicle. Engines, transmissions, tires, they all take a beating pulling the ups and downs of Appalachia. Over time I noticed that my engine was skipping as I drove over the bigger mountains. It seemed that it was lacking power. This continued until I couldn't take it any longer and could barely make it up hills. I had the issue diagnosed and found four cylinders were out on my truck, they had to be replaced.

When Jesus told his disciples to wait until they were endued with power in Acts 1:8, he knew their efforts would be hindered without full power. Just like my truck trying to go over the big mountains at half power. It made it over, but it was a much harder go than it should have been. I've lived life with no spiritual power, lived it at half power, and lived it walking empowered by the Spirit to see God's will fulfilled in my life. I can tell you from experience the latter is best. So how do we get there?

First, remove any hindrance that might be in your life. If there is pride, it needs to go, perhaps besetting sin, it must be given to God. Pray and ask the Lord to reveal anything that stands between you and the power of God active in your life. Second, immerse yourself in the things of God, and surround yourself with Godly friends. Listen to worship music as you drive, read the word instead of the newspaper, fast a few meals, spend lunch break in prayer. Immerse yourself in the things of God. Finally, just open yourself up to the possibilities of heaven. Telling the Lord, if there is greater anointing you want it, if there is a deeper walk you are willing, whatever the Lord calls you to do you'll do it.

The Lord's command in Acts was for the Apostles. However, I would note that Acts appears to be free from an ending statement. We were never told to stop doing what the church began doing. As a believer it is our duty to receive from God, and then give what we have to those around us. Walk in power.

LESSON 17
GROW WHERE YOU'RE PLANTED

Only let each person lead the life that the
Lord has assigned to him, and to which
God has called him.

— 1 CORINTHIANS 7:17 ESV

Down the road from Shady Valley, partway between our home and Damascus, VA is our family's favorite relaxation spot. Officially it's named Backbone Rock Recreation Area, but we refer to it simply as Backbone Rock. The rock is a seventy-five-foot tall, fourteen-foot-wide rock. Around 1901 engineers with the Beaver Dam/Shady Valley railroad decided that track could not be laid around the rock, the best course of action was to go right through, thus they created what is known as the world's shortest tunnel. The main reason for the railroad to come in was the timber industry. Today Shady Valley is mostly farmland and cattle grazing down in the valley. But in the early days it was completely covered by forests, that's how they came by the name shady. The timber industry began drying up around 1917 and the railroad tracks were removed making way for a road to run through the tunnel.[1] Today the recreation area boasts a campground, a hiking trail that spans across the top of the rock, over the tunnel, and crosses the road, a pit toilet, trout fishing, rock climbing, picnic tables, grills, and a couple small shelters. The trail also connects to the Appalachian Trail a few miles shy of Damascus, Virginia; Backbone Rock is a wonderful place.

We love visiting this area and taking friends there. As hikers pass through our area, we hope to offer reprieve and fellowship to those we have connected with. We figure Backbone rock is a nice place to hang out. On one particular trip with friends, I made an observation. One of the old picnic shelters has a roofing issue. Not an issue that made it unstable or caused it to leak. The wooden tiles that made up the roof had years of moss growing over them. This moss provided a base layer where small pines were growing out of the top of the roof. I walked around the structure and noticed some of these were as high as four feet. "Wow, I can't believe those are growing up there," I mumbled to myself. Then one of the truths of life came flooding back into my memory. You must grow where you're planted. These small pines had done a wonderful job of growing in spite of never touching the ground. This was not a normal place for a tree to grow, not normal circumstances, but nonetheless they were growing there on the roof.

I know we sometimes wonder about our own lives. How did I get here from there? Are we happy with our lives? Are we making the most of the opportunities God has given us each day? Growing where we are planted is more than a catchy aphorism. It's a part of our everyday lives. If we are Christians, then we know that Psalms 37 says God ordains the steps of the righteous. If God is in control, and ordains our steps, then we must believe that the place we find ourselves today is ordained of God. It is easy to become disheartened when we feel our plans haven't worked out. Remembering this helps put aside the lies of the enemy concerning our lives.

Soren Kierkegaard says, "Life can only be understood backwards, but must be lived forwards." Looking back, I see so many instances where I had plans, I had dreams, and they didn't go the way I wanted them to go. Becoming a minister was not in my original plan, and the Appalachian Trail was nowhere on my rader. I recently ran into a friend I hadn't seen in years. He was very inquisitive about our work on the trail, most are. I asked him, "If I told you twenty years ago, Brad would become a brain surgeon or a missionary to the Appalachian Trail. Which would you say was more likely?" His reply, "I'd have to say brain surgeon." We both had a laugh at that, but here's the deal, we must be able to grow where God leads us. The adage is true, sometimes I thank God for unanswered prayers, or the prayers he said no to. At the time it was a crushing blow to me, to see my plans erased, relationships falter, life forcing me left when I wanted to go right. Looking back, I see the plan and hand of God in each step. It was as if some unseen hand was guiding me to this place. Things I went through and wondered why I had to walk through that season, I now look back on and realize I was learning something useful for my present ministry.

I have an exercise that I find helps me to appreciate where I am presently and fosters new growth in this place. First, remember where you came from. I'm a packrat by nature. I literally will not get rid of anything. If you've given me a note, letter, or card, in the last twenty years there's a good chance I still have it. I have a "feel good" file. I put all the notes in the feel-good file and when I'm feeling down, I go read them. In that file are some letters we had to write while seniors in high school. Where do you see yourself in ten years, twenty years, the list goes on? Did I do the work I said I'd do? Nope. Did I marry whatever girl I was crushing on at the time? Absolutely not. But looking back I can see how far I've come, how I've matured, how what I thought was important, really isn't that important. Fame is not important; money is not important. The old timers have a saying that rings so true, I may not be where I wanted to be, but I'm thankful to the Lord I'm not where I was. The Lord has brought this ole boy a mighty long way, and I'm happy where I am, remembering where he brought me from.

Another thought that helps me in my present place of growth is knowing that somebody is currently praying to be where I am. How can I be depressed in this place where I'm planted when 690 million people go to be undernourished each night.[2] That's twice the population of the United States. If you are reading this most likely you have living conditions that over a billion people would gladly trade places with. Yet we feel so depressed at times in our current situations. When I was younger, I asked myself the question, "why me?" Why don't I have all the best things, drive the best car, and have the most respectable family? I have learned the proper question is, "why not me?" Why not me born in sub-Saharan Africa in the middle of a three-year drought, why not me living in a war-torn nation in a civil war, why not me growing up in a closed, cut off, society with no access to the gospel. We tend to make our small problems seem big, while making others' big problems seem small. Be thankful every day for how good you have it.

Finally, thankful, joyful people grow no matter what soil they are planted in. Our attitude, and the way we see the world has everything to do with our growth. Our goals should be to grow spiritually, to become better parents, to leave the world better than we found it, to leave a legacy. If we constantly walk through life with a bad attitude, none of these things will happen. John Milton, in his famous work Paradise Lost writes, "The mind is its own place, and in itself can make a heaven of hell, or a hell of heaven." [3] Dale Carnegie put it this way, "Two men looked out from prison bars, One saw mud, the other saw stars." [4] Life, and the situations you find yourself in are what you allow the Lord to make it.

Paul and Silas are excellent examples of this principle; growing where you're planted. They had been busy with the Lord's work but were arrested for preaching Jesus. They had been beaten, the skin on their backs broken open with blows, and then thrown into a Philippian jail. This would have been an unsanitary, filthy environment, with potential for infection in open wounds, plus they were now shackled, locked into this nastiness. Acts 16 records something amazing. It says around midnight Paul and Silas were praying, and worshiping, and all the prisoners were listening to them. Suddenly the ground shakes, the shackles fall off, and the prison doors swing open. I don't believe the earthquake that freed them was the greatest thing in the story, their worship and praise in the middle of this situation was the most amazing thing. It goes contrary to human nature. They were planted in this horrible place, and they grew there, not just them, the kingdom grew there. The other prisoners saw this, and the jailer. Ultimately the jailer and his whole family believed and were saved.

The amazing thing about growth is nobody grows in a vacuum. When we grow, our kids grow, our friends grow. There were multiple trees growing on that old roof. One taller and the others sprouting up around it. Once that first one got a root system in the moss, it was easier for the other trees to grow in this abnormal place. You remember where you came from, realize all you have, carry a thankful, joyous attitude, and watch you and the world around you flourish.

LESSON 18
THE MOUNTAINS ARE CALLING

For since the creation of the world His invisible attributes are clearly seen, being understood by the things that are made, even His eternal power and Godhead, so that they are without excuse.

— ROMANS 1:20 NKJV

It was a beautiful day in the Shenandoah mountains of central Virginia. The Trail Servants crew, composed mainly of our family, was set up ministering to the needs of hikers on this warm summer day. Hikers come in many shapes and sizes, with varying reasons for starting the trail. Many are in transitional phases of life. By transitional phase we are speaking of the time between high school and college, or college and a first job, but many times people have lost a business, lost a spouse or significant person, retired, there are many transitional phases in life, and any reasons for being on trail. Some are trying to find themselves in the wilderness, others try to lose themselves there. This day we ran into a couple that had found each other along the Appalachian Trail.

Bullfrog and Angel were a memorable couple, and our encounter with them led to a unique experience. They didn't know each other pre hike but had joined up hiking together north of Hot Springs, North Carolina. By the time we met them in Virginia they were fully smitten with each other, and today they are married, but I'm jumping ahead of the story. Bullfrog and Angel strolled up and immediately we hit it off, their company was enjoyable. As we shared drinks and snacks, they asked who we were, this usually comes up in conversation. I explained we were missionaries working with hikers along the Appalachian Trail. We reach out, show love, encourage, and try to be the hands and feet of Jesus. Angel suddenly jumped up and ran to her pack, she dug around for a few seconds, and returned with travel communion cups. I was pleasantly surprised to see this and asked her how she got that way out in the middle of nowhere. She explained her mom had sent them to her in a package from home and they'd been traveling with her waiting on the right time, and this was the right time. Wow, communion on the Appalachian Trail, I can't for sure say this was a first for the trail, most likely it wasn't, but it was a first for us.

This was the most informal communion service of my life, but I'm fine with that. I've learned that I'm more the informal type, and taking communion without having showered for days, wearing shorts and a t-shirt, on a mountainside, might be the most Christ-like communion service I'd ever experienced. We need to realize most of the miracles listed in the Bible happen outside of the synagogue. The things we assume happen in church, were never made just for the four walls of a church. John the Baptist dunked people in a river, Paul engaged townspeople in the marketplace, Jesus taught from hillsides. I've had hikers ask me where my church was located, and I tell them "You're standing in it."

John Muir famously said, "the mountains are calling, and I must go." This saying is known around the world, it's on t-shirts, bumper stickers, and coffee cups. But what is it about mountains and wild spaces that call to the inner parts of mankind? It's as if there is something intrinsic about time spent in nature. Even the busiest cities allow room for green spaces, knowing that they can become places of solitude and healing for city dwellers consumed with the hustle and bustle of life.

Every year the draw of the wilderness brings millions of people into outdoor spaces. Of these millions, I've encountered many who would say they're hoping for a spiritual experience. In fact, some of the first "long distance hikers" were pilgrims who walked long distances to religious shrines. Today the Camino de Santiago is a long-distance trail in Spain, with routes extending into parts of Portugal and France. These routes trace religious pilgrimages that date back to the Middle Ages. So, it has been throughout the history of humankind that we have ventured into the wilderness in search of peace, inspiration, cleansing, wholeness, and communion with our creator.

A well-traveled section hiker once said the wilderness reaffirmed her belief in God's presence. It gave her hope, and a deeper appreciation for her family and friends, while bringing out the best of who she was.[1] Many hikers come to the trail with an idea of faith, some attend church regularly back home, while the majority are closer to the fringes of belief in a higher power. Those who have a regular prayer life at home often report feeling a rejuvenation of communication with walking through the mountains.

The wilderness served many purposes in scripture. Moses ran to the "backside of the desert," the children of Israel wandered in the wilderness for forty years, John the Baptist preached repentance in the wilderness, and Jesus spent forty days in the wilderness. These are just a few of the over three hundred mentions of the wilderness in scripture. People spending time in, finding purpose in, and having a renewed sense of life's calling in the wilderness is nothing new.

My friend Boxcar is one of the most unique, and interesting people I know. He has rode trains, lived under bridges, authored books about his life, hiked thousands of miles, and ultimately found solace in the mountains. He has started an organization called Trails of Recovery where he hopes to share his testimony of renewal that began on the hiking trails of North America. For him hiking began to open the door to a life free from the constraints of addiction. Ultimately culminating in him finding salvation through Christ, but this journey towards Christ started years before we met in early 2020, it started with him hiking, seeing the wonder of creation, clearing his mind of the confusion life constantly throws our way. His goal is to share this with others who are hurting and struggling with addiction. So, it seems that while the mountains call to man, the mountains also help facilitate God's call to man.

Our headlining scripture from Romans points to there being no excuse in regards to knowing God. Even though God is invisible and unseen, the work of the creator is all around us. The giant sequoias rise like spires of a grand temple toward the heavens, waterfalls cascade over rocks with the sound of a grand chorus, the birds join in unison forming a boisterous choir. You sit with wonder among this creation, and the questions wind through your mind. Is it possible this all happened by chance?

I remember the story of an archeologist working in the desert. The dig was hard, and hot, ultimately turning up several clay pots with intricate designs painted on the sides. These were remarkable for two reasons, one was their pristine condition, the other was the unique design. The archeologist, an atheist, was asked about the formation of the pots, he said they were evidence that a skilled craftsman and worked tirelessly to make the pots. A Christian colleague later challenged him with this question, "You affirm that the pots needed a craftsman, are you willing to affirm the natural world, which is hundreds of times more complex than the pot, needs a craftsman?" When we look at the intricate designs, the craftsmanship of nature, the ebb and flow of tides, we simply are without excuse.

Nature, mountains, the wilderness, I have used these terms somewhat interchangeably. The point is this, in many aspects of the natural world, we see characteristics of God, our creator. Ezekiel and John the Revelator both confirm that the voice of God was as the sound of many waters. If you've ever stood beside a large waterfall, you understand the rumble, the booming sound, that in this spectacle of nature, you see a quality of God. Perhaps you've stood on a massive mountain overlook, the ones that stretch as far as you can see, without a road crossing, or another person. In that moment you feel a closeness to God, and begin to grasp the vastness, the greatness, of God.

If you heard me speak in the early days of support gathering, you no doubt heard me tell the story of a hiker, suffering from the loss of his brother. This fellow had planned to hike with his brother before his tragic death. He admitted that he was not particularly religious, but in the middle of his hike, dealing with grief, standing on a mountain overlook, he realized there must be something more to life. That there must be some higher power, a creator. Yes, it's true the mountains are calling, and hopefully people grasp what that call is about. It's not just the seen, but the unseen, it's not the waterfall, but the one with a voice of many waters, calling out, reaching out, desiring the heart of mankind.

LESSON 19
HOPE DEALERS

For surely there is a hereafter, and your hope
will not be cut off.

— PROVERBS 23:18 NKJV

Hope is a feeling, an expectation for the future. When we begin a new job, we hope it will be better than our old job. We hope that one year will be better than the last or have more opportunities than the last year. Hikers begin walking in Georgia with the hope of making Katahdin, or whatever predetermined spot on the map they have selected. Many are dealing with issues they hope will resolve as they travel through the ridges and green tunnels of the trail. I've already mentioned those going through transitional phases of life as a catalyst for hiking. Many of the transitions have left people devoid of hope. So it is my goal, as a minister among these masses, to offer hope. People who are hurting, alienated, marginalized, and have enough people throwing rocks their way. We need Christians willing to throw ropes not rocks. Ropes to help lift the spirits of another, to help uplift a weary soul, to help another out of the pit of despair.

There is a world outside your door that needs hope. Someone needs that message.

It's unfortunate that suicide is an emerging problem among hikers. It seems every year the number grows, five one year, seven the next, and so on. The community has taken notice, almost every hiker knows someone personally who felt hopeless enough in their current situation to take their own life. My first year on trail I met a cool hiker in Georgia. He was in the middle of a YoYo hike, this means he hiked the trail up, and when he got to Maine he immediately turned and went back to Georgia. Basically, a back-to-back through hike; over four thousand miles of hiking. He was so acclimated to sleeping outside that he didn't even use a tent. The morning after I met him, I climbed out of my tent to find him and his dog sleeping on a piece of cardboard curled up by the fire. He had a big smile, he was the life of the party, he didn't meet a stranger, and was just as comfortable talking to the Chaplain as he was talking to anyone else. I ran into him a second time in Damascus, VA at Trail Days in 2019. There is usually a theme and somehow the 2019 theme involved the guys wearing dresses or women's attire. My buddy didn't choose to wear a dress, he instead opted for a romper, a very thin romper. He walked along happily near the back of the hiker parade with his dog. Later I found him by the river in town, he ran over and gave me a big hug in his romper, wet from a recent swim. I've since sworn off receiving hugs from men in wet rompers, it doesn't leave much to the imagination. Michelle took a picture of him and his girlfriend for him. I genuinely enjoyed his company; I wish I had known it was the last time I'd see my friend.

He moved to Colorado after finishing the YoYo hike. I had a few friends there who knew him, he'd occasionally show up in their pictures, he seemed to be fine, but I'd lost touch with him. It can be hard to stay in contact with nomads who don't always wish to be found. In the summer of 2020, I looked at my phone after a long day of hiking in North Carolina, I was shocked by what I saw. It was a picture of my friend, and at the bottom of the picture was two dates: one marking the beginning of his life, and one marking the end. I sat and cried. I cried because I felt I'd failed him. I wondered what brought him to the point of ending his life, how did I miss the signs? Everyone who knew him shared photos online, in every picture he was happy, the life of the party, the care-free soul who never had a bad day, the guy who had a soft spot for the missionary.

I called and broke the news to Michelle; she was equally taken aback. She sent me several pictures we had taken at Trail Days. Later his sister requested pictures from his travels if anyone had them. I sent several including one of him walking his dog in a romper at Trail Days. The lingering questions remained, what could we have done differently, and what can we do in the future?

I have found a few things to be true, and I'll share them with you.

The key to bringing hope to others is always letting them know you bring hope without judgment. People who are hurting often feel they are being watched, judged, or accused even if these are completely unwarranted feelings. They put up good fronts and carry smiles to disguise the pain. It happens on hiking trails, in the office, at church, and anywhere else you find people. Hope Dealers must offer love without judgment, the world has plenty of the latter, and not enough of the former. You can never help someone you look down on. The story of Jesus and the woman caught in adultery, described in John 8 is a great example. He never defended her actions, but he told her he didn't condemn her. We only see two options, affirmation or alienation, Jesus did neither of these. To walk with someone between affirmation and alienation, offering hope, is a great challenge of contemporary ministry.

Another point is consistency. We must consistently share love, share the gospel, and be an open shoulder to lean on. Anyone who is struggling needs stability, not someone who loves them one minute, and flies off the handle another. We can't attempt to care, and then gossip about the situation. The only way to be found trustworthy to offer hope is to be consistent in your care for another.

I've learned that when it comes to the subject of anxiety, depression, and a plethora of mental struggles, how little I know about these struggles. Not how little

I'm affected by these, because I'm human and I recognize that I have my days, just ask my wife. However, I'm not a professional counselor, I can offer advice, I can share the Gospel, I can help you find a professional counselor, but I'm not the last stop for the train.

As ministers, for years there has been a stigma towards mental health professionals. We must understand that "just pray about it," while solid advice, is not the answer in every individual's situation. Finding a qualified counselor that you trust and being able to recommend a qualified counselor that you trust, does not show lack of faith. It is no different than referring a friend to speak with your doctor for a second opinion. Many organizations, denominations, and groups are now moving towards having qualified professionals available, but then the kicker is removing the stigma, so people get help.

I know ministers who feel that going to a counselor will be perceived as a sign of weakness and recommending professional help to a congregant is a lack of faith and power. Ministers burn out daily, over fifteen hundred a month leave their positions, receiving help when it's needed is not weakness. If you are a minister, or congregant reading this, and you are struggling, you are not alone and there is help.

The interaction of Jesus with a blind man in John 9:6 (NKJV) speaks volumes to me. It says, "When He had said these things, He spat on the ground and made clay with saliva; and He anointed the eyes of the blind man with the clay. And He said to him, "Go, wash in the pool of Siloam." So, he went and washed and came back. This speaks to me because in this healing we see a mixture of the natural world, and the supernatural world at work. The Savior uses the dirt of the ground as part of the miracle, and usually miracles work that way, part dirt, part divine. If a doctor is used in my healing, God does not get less glory. If a therapist, a counselor, is used, God does not get less glory. It's just a mix of the dirt and divine working to heal the hurting.

Ultimately, all my hope is in Jesus, and to show hope is to show Jesus. When I was growing up, I was taught how to share Jesus with others. We'd go to someone's house, sit on the couch, engage in a short conversation, and then flatly ask them if they died today would they go to heaven. I genuinely believe we had the best intentions; this was a tried and proven method among evangelicals. Basically, "do you know Jesus?" This was the Bible belt after all, it was a safe question, everybody "knew Jesus." It was easy, it didn't require getting our hands dirty if people knew Jesus, good. If not that's okay, we'd plead our case, and if you weren't convinced, we'd mark you down to see again in six months. Did we really try to understand their struggles? What were their kids dealing with? Are their basic needs covered, can we help with anything around the house? It's not that churches I've been involved with didn't do these things, but at times we went in guns blazing offering Jesus or Hell. That's a much more consequential decision for a Tuesday evening than whether you should buy the Rainbow vacuum, but I always ended up feeling like a vacuum salesman.

Recently I sat down with a fellow who was walking cross country. He was hiking to the Gulf of Mexico and needed help one day, and that's what I do. I help hikers. Once we got to his room, and he got settled, we went out to dinner. I talked about being a Chaplain to hikers and he mentioned that several times on his walk people had stopped to offer him assistance and flatly asked if he knew Jesus. He said anytime this happened it was an automatic turnoff. I laughed. I knew this was the way many people felt.

It's been years since I handed someone a gospel tract. I do use an app to keep up with hikers, but these are usually individuals I've sat with, I've built rapport with, we have a relationship, and this is the key. Hope Dealers cultivate relationships. It's not a quick few minutes of your time asking if you know Jesus. It's showing the love of Jesus in tangible ways. It's investing in the life of another, no strings attached. You can't enter a friendship with an agenda. I will admit, this is hard for someone raised like I was. We are hardwired to seal the deal, get them to pray a prayer, the old sales adage, "Always Be Closing." Please know this, people aren't projects that we discard if they don't believe or behave as we wish. First, just be a friend. Stats show that less than 5% of Christians regularly spend time with "unchurched" friends. The most common reason a person comes to a church event is a friend invites them. If you're not friendly, your invitation typically falls on deaf ears. You can't change a soul, the pressure is not on you, you don't save anyone. Only God can do that. Our job is a relationship, it's modeling the hope we have in Christ Jesus, God's job is to save.

Once you have developed a friendship, just be available, without fail hard times come. Life is messy, but you must be a friend in good times and bad. The world is full of fair-weather friends, don't be those people. In the hard moments of life, when you're still there, when you really care for the needs of another, God does amazing things.

LESSON 20
THE WAY

*Jesus said to him, "I am the way, the truth,
and the life. No one comes to the Father
except through me.*

— JOHN 14:6 NKJV

Knowing the way is an extremely important aspect of hiking. Millions of dollars are spent yearly by aspiring thru hikers on apps and guidebooks which show you the way. For sure nobody wants to be lost in the wilderness, not only is this an uncomfortable thought, but it can also be deadly. There are areas of America's wilderness so vast that planes have crashed, and even though radar shows the general area of the crash, they took years to be located. Staying found in the backcountry is imperative.

Trails are marked with blazes. These are typically

two by six-inch stripes painted on trees, but can be small metal signs, or other designs. Each of the blazes are color coded to mark the trail. For instance, the Appalachian Trail is marked with a white blaze, the Florida Trail has orange blazes, and trails leading to water are marked with a blue blaze. If you venture more than a few hundred feet along these trails without seeing a blaze that is a bad sign, you need to turn around because most likely you have missed the correct path.

I was hiking once along the Appalachian Trail and was certain I was on the right path. However, there is a fine line between a hiking path and a game trail. As I hiked, I noticed all the things I love about the woods, the sun shining through the trees, the bright salamanders that scurried under rocks as you passed, the massive trees, but then I noticed the lack of blazes. I had been so captivated with the beauty of the forest that I missed the actual trail. I backtracked about a hundred fifty yards until I found the turn in the trail where I lost the path. Even with the guidebooks, and best apps, you will still lose your way from time to time.

Just as on a trail the most important thing in our spiritual life is to find the proper way, stay on that path, and help others find the way. If we're going to show the way to others, we must first know the way ourselves. We recreate what we are, and if we're not where we need to be on our walk, it's unfortunate that others will follow us down the wrong road. I've seen hikers in groups blindly following the person out front in the wrong direction.

Who are you leading? Who is following you? These are things we need to think about. We are all leading someone down a path in this life.

There is a great story found in Acts 8. The Spirit ushered Philip into the desert, and there he encountered an Ethiopian who was reading from the book of Isaiah. Philip asked him if he understood what he was reading. I love verse 35 which says Philip began at the scripture the Ethiopian was reading and taught him from there. If we're going to lead anyone in the path of Christ, we must start where they are. I remember leading Bible school classes for fifth and sixth graders years ago. We had a great time learning basic biblical principles, but my biggest challenge in teaching was getting on their level. Always be mindful of where people are and understand that people growing up outside of the church see things far differently. This is a lesson it's taken me some time to learn, and a hard one at that.

If you are going to show the way you must be able to start where another is and move them forward, but what if that means unlearning the churchisms and language you've been taught your whole life. Talking about being "washed in the blood" with someone who has never been to church, and has no knowledge of scripture, can be extremely confusing. Can you share the gospel conversationally? The world is not looking for King James English, it's looking for someone who can naturally share who Christ is and what he means to you. Sharing the good news is not that complicated. Recently,

I was eating with a group of hikers, and someone noticed the sticker on my phone. It's a sticker for my friend's book, "*When Jesus Stole My Bread*." The hiker asked what that meant, which allowed me to tell the story of Jesus and the miraculous feeding of the five thousand. It was a nice conversation, and the gospel was shared; when we meet people where they are amazing things happen.

Another great example of this is found in the book *Bruchko* by Bruce Olson. This true story is a missionary masterpiece and I highly recommend the book. Olson tells of his encounters with native tribes, specifically the Motilone Bari Indians of Columbia and Venezuela. Other missionaries came and tried to evangelize the Motilone, but they also brought various Western traditions. They told Indians they couldn't live communally in circular houses but had to live in square houses. They tried to do away with the traditional forms of dress, trading in the loin cloth for pants and shirts. Olson, with no formal training, chose not to implement these restrictions. It wasn't a sin to live in a circular hut, nor was it a sin to dress traditionally. He taught the local witch doctor to administer medicine, rather than him losing his role in tribal society. Bruce did what few missionaries had been able to do, he befriended the local witch doctor to show him Christ. Most importantly, Olson took some of the native origin stories and simply injected the truth of scripture. He used examples of them walking the paths in the jungle for walking the way of Jesus. He started where they were and moved them forward.[1]

I don't want to get technical, if you've read this far you've figured out, I'm a simple fellow. I always preach and teach with transformation in mind, not information. Someone else can teach you Hebrew and Greek, I'm more worried about how you live, and how you love people. However, I want to take a moment and mention showing the way in a postmodern context. Postmodern meaning sharing the gospel with people born 1980-present. First, you need to know that postmodernism believes that absolute truth is impossible. We know Jesus is the way, and the truth. We believe scripture is the truth, and individuals born in earlier times could be convinced of truth simply by you telling them. Postmodernism does not care for stated truth; they want to know what is real. Let me give an example. Someone born in the 1960's hears a sermon on healing, they feel it is the truth, may not have seen it, but know it's true. Another person born in the late 1990's hears you talking about healing, that's nice, you believe what you believe, I'm not fully convinced. You have your truth; they have their truth. But when you pray for a swollen ankle, or a hurt knee, that's real. When they're up walking around the next day, that's real. You can't just tell them Jesus loved the poor and needy, they must see you love the poor and needy, that's real. If your desire is to minister in a postmodern context you must be real.

If you want to minister to postmoderns, you must know this truth. For Postmoderns, tolerance is seen as the greatest virtue one can have, and intolerance is seen as repulsive. So this is where loving and leading like Jesus requires diligence and work. It's too easy to say we won't have that here, not in this church, oh no, no. Back to the women caught in adultery. Jesus perfectly walked the fine line and showed compassion, without sacrificing truth. The intolerant crowd had to drop their stones and sulk home. Jesus touched lepers, ate meals with sinners, and prostitutes washed his feet with their tears. He wasn't tolerant with no end result in mind, but he was tolerant, loving, and this combined with him being real, walking in power, changed their lives forever.[2]

Many people in our world today are fragile. Life can be ruff, I'm very breakable at times. In the old days ministers could just go in guns blazing. I have been a practitioner of this form of ministry, it's fun, it's loud, it works in Alabama, but everywhere is not Alabama. We must also be able to holster our guns and put on kid gloves and handle people with care. We must handle people like we handle the priceless family ornaments when we take them off the Christmas tree. Unfortunately, most of the time we end up being the cat that runs in and topples the whole tree over, breaking everything in its path. Handling with care does not come easy for me, it's not natural for me, but I'm thankful for the growth process the Lord has taken me through.

We must know the way, and properly know how to show the way. Remember, there are seven billion different, unique people on this planet at any given moment. We each minister to people from different places, in different social constructs, and what I have given are suggestions based on my experience. There is no perfect model, but instruction done in love, while walking in power, seems to have worked for Jesus. Whatever method you choose to show the way, it can never be divorced from love. I'll leave it at that.

LESSON 21
HOW MUCH DO YOU REALLY NEED?

A devout life does bring wealth, but it's the
rich simplicity of being yourself before
God. Since we entered the world penni-
less and will leave it penniless, if we have
bread on the table and shoes on our feet,
that's enough.

— 1 TIMOTHY 6:6-8 MSG

One of the great discoveries that new hikers make each year is the ability to live with much less than our modern world needs to survive. They realize how much stuff they don't need. Surviving for six months with nothing but the clothes on their back, the shoes on their feet, their shelter, and what little food they carry. Usually, this conversation kicks up around Pennsylvania. That's the area when it really begins to sink in, that you don't need most of the stuff that life has conditioned you to believe you need.

It's not unusual for hikers to go home, put all their stuff out at a yard sale, buy a van or a camper, and decide to live a simple existence. I know tons of people who have done this. I joke that I never thought I'd know so many people who lived in their cars. It takes a little finagling on the east coast, but out west is a different story. Out west you have public land, sometimes 40% of the state is public land. Alaska is 95% public land, Utah is 75%, Colorado is 43%. If you are curious, Alabama is only 7% public land.[1] In the western states, you can drive out, set up camp off a forest service road, and generally stay in that spot for two weeks. At the end of two weeks, you must move, but you might just move a half-mile down the road and reset the clock.

The last few years have taught me much about what you really need in life. Not just what we need, but what we don't need, and how much of our lives are consumed by excess, especially in North America. I am no stranger to excess, I spent a large portion of my adult life trying to make a buck, pursuing the American dream; I went back to school and earned an M.B.A. in Accounting, and was a Controller for a company before I got that good insurance job. I've flipped houses, and worked with investments, believe me, I know something about chasing the wind. The question then is how does that line up biblically with how we are called to live? I will say I have nothing against money. Many people misquote 1

Timothy 6:10 and say money is the root of evil, money is not the root of evil, the "love" of money is the root of evil according to Timothy. I'm a missionary and missionaries need money; God's work requires money. I hope all my friends are successful, I pray for their business ventures, but we must keep it in perspective.

Some of you may remember the short story by Leo Tolstoy "How Much Land Does a Man Require." The main character is a peasant farmer named Pahom. Pahom believes more land and a bigger farm would be the key to a successful life. He moves his family to a bigger commune and begins to amass wealth, but he is farming rented land, so he strives to buy his own land. Finally, he is introduced to the Bashkirs who own much land. They make him a simple, but unique, bargain. For the sum of one thousand rubles, Pahom can have as much land as he can walk around from sunrise until sunset. The catch is if he is not back at the original starting point by sunset, he would get no land and lose his money. He believes he can cover a great deal of distance and get much land; this is an amazing deal. At sunrise he sets off, but towards the evening he realizes he is far away from the starting point. He runs as fast as he can and makes it back to the starting point just as the sun sets, sealing the land deal. Then he collapses and dies from exhaustion. They bury Pahom in a 6ft x 4ft plot. So, how much land does a man really need? [2]

Perhaps it's easy for me to question excess, I've been fortunate to know little of it most of my life. I feel part of my calling as a minister is to get people to think, to push against the status quo, to make myself and others uncomfortable, to deal with hard issues. I told my wife I would purposefully put this lesson near the end of the book, because most people will have placed it on a nightstand or bookshelf before they get to this chapter; very few will read it. It's controversial, but here's the deal, we need to understand what's important in life, and it's not money and stuff. I wish I could sit every young father down and tell them not to miss a t-ball game trying to pay for a 2500 HD pickup. We buy things we don't need, to impress people we don't like, with money we don't have. I remember once I worked all day on Saturday as an accountant, I left work at five p.m. and ran home to attend my birthday party with my family and went right back to work until around ten p.m. so we could close the month's books. I was pastoring a church at the same time. This was the day I realized something had to change.

Jesus has an interesting discussion with his disciples in the Synoptic Gospels, meaning Matthew, Mark, and Luke. He mentions it would be easier for a camel to go through the eye of a needle, than for a rich man to enter heaven. There are a couple different ways to look at it. One, the Pharisees and Rabbis really liked hanging out with rich people, and they taught that the rich were blessed by God. These obviously were the people pleasing God, and thus making heaven. Jesus wanted to strip that notion away, there is no way to earn heaven, you can't buy your way in, earthly treasures mean little to the God who owns the cattle on a thousand hills. If you're blessed with wealth, fine, it rains on the just and the unjust, but don't see it as a special perk of pleasing God.

The other school of thought has a more literal meaning. Jesus used an illustration of a camel because it was the largest land animal in Israel. There was said to be a narrow gate in the wall of Jerusalem which remained open after the main gate closed. The only way for a camel to enter here was to strip all the excess baggage off the animal, and have it crawl through the opening on its knees. Not an easy task. It's not that a rich person wouldn't be able to get in, but there might be things like pride, greed, excess things that need to be stripped away. But I really want us to focus on the word rich. Who are these rich people? We know who they are: Bill Gates, Elon Musk, and Mark Cuban. These are the wicked ole rich people, right? What if I told you, the rich are you and I.? If you have food in your refrigerator, clothes on your back, a roof over your head, and a place to sleep, then you are richer than 75% of this world. If you have a little money in the bank, in your wallet, and change in a dish, you are among the top 8% of the world's wealthiest people. If you can attend any religious or political meeting you want without fear of imprisonment or persecution, you have it better than three billion people. If you are reading this book, you are ahead of one billion people who cannot read across the planet. I pray we rich folks can throw off the baggage and get on our knees.

You see, we have a responsibility. I love the quote

from Spiderman, "to whom much is given, much is required." I'm not trying to beat up the church. Churches across America do innumerable good deeds, from recovery programs to soup kitchens, after-school care to foster care programs, and everything in between. The church in America literally contributes billions, but Cain's failure wasn't that he didn't bring an offering; his failure was he didn't bring his best. If every church and Christian in America gave their best to missions, gave their best to addicts, gave their best to the homeless, gave their best to reach the lost in their community, we'd turn this place upside down. If we gave the best of our time, the best of our talents, we could see revival if we got serious about offering our first fruits to the Lord. What if what we call radical obedience, God calls normal, and what we call normal Christian living, God calls unacceptable? I hear about the rapture all the time, but if we really believed what we preached, that time is growing short, we wouldn't stockpile stuff; we would give all we had to see His kingdom come. At the risk of being hit in the head with a rock by my "brothers and sisters," I ask you to examine your life, examine your church, and let's examine our hearts.

I have a favorite story that perfectly illustrates giving your best. I spoke at a church one Sunday night. They took up a love offering for our missions work at the end of the service. Some gave $20, some gave $100, but as I left the church, a young man stopped me and handed me $1.90 in dimes. Nineteen dimes. He told me he was a new believer and had only been attending the church for a couple of months. My friend said he was embarrassed to put such a small sum in the offering plate but felt compelled to give it to me. It was every dime he and his wife had. I told him not to be embarrassed, that he had given more than anyone else because he gave all he had to offer. I still have that $1.90 in a little bag on my desk. I figure if I ever go completely bust, I'll still have that $1.90, and I always want to remember his sacrificial gift.

An interesting side note to this story. I ran into the young man a couple weeks later. He said the day he gave me the $1.90, he owed a $60 water bill that he couldn't pay. He figured if he didn't have the bill money, it didn't matter if he trusted the Lord and gave the last he had; it wasn't enough to pay the bill anyway. Then a few days later, he received a shock. A lady came to him and handed him $60; she told him she felt led by the Lord to do so. She didn't know anything about his bill or the giving of his last dime to missions. So you see, the Lord promises no riches, but he does take care of his own; he bends his ear to the faithful.

Time is your most valuable commodity. The time you spend serving the Lord, that you spend with the people you love, that you spend serving others, this is what really matters in the end. Remember what true riches really are. Someone once said real wealth is found in what you have that money can't buy.

Finally, in Matthew 6:19-21, Jesus tells us not to lay up treasures on earth but to lay them in heaven where rust and rot can't destroy them. He goes on to say where your treasure is, there your heart is. Is it wrong to have stuff and to enjoy things? I don't think so. We have stuff, but we need to ensure our stuff doesn't have us. Make the most of your time, give your best, lay up treasure in heaven, and enjoy your eternal reward.

LESSON 22

IT'S NOT TOO LATE TO CHASE YOUR DREAMS

Wisdom is with the aged, and with length of days comes understanding.

— JOB 12:12 NKJV

C.S. Lewis once said, "You are never too old to set a new goal or dream a new dream," and I tend to believe him. I like to tell people that I plan to go back into youth ministry when I turn sixty. You laugh, but if you really know me, you know I'm only partly kidding. If there is one thing the trail has taught me, it's that it's never too late to pursue your dreams. I've been blessed to meet many amazing hikers on the trails of America, and some of my favorites are much older than me. If you meet someone whose zeal for life is unabated, whose passion grows with each passing year, and who refuses to quit, you should spend time with that person. You should learn everything you can from that person, and you will find one message comes through clear: it's never too late.

In 2019 an eighty-seven-year-old Victor Kubilius, also known as Pappy, became the oldest person to attempt the Appalachian Trail. He completed hundreds of miles, falling a couple hundred miles short of a thru-hike. He already held the record as the oldest triple crown hiker, meaning he completed the Appalachian Trail, the Continental Divide Trail, and the Pacific Crest Trail. That's a fantastic accomplishment at any age, but at seventy-one years of age, it was epic. Then, in 2021 Meredith Eberhart, known as Nimblewill Nomad, became the oldest hiker to complete the entire Appalachian Trail at eighty-three. He started his hike on the Pinhoti Trail in Northeast Alabama, so he hiked more than the traditional Appalachian Trail mileage. Also, there is the famous George "Billy Goat" Woodard. Billy Goat has hiked more than fifty thousand miles over forty years. The astounding thing is he didn't start thru-hiking long trails until his mid-forties when he retired from rail-road work. One of the most accomplished hikers of his generation didn't begin long-distance hiking until retirement! Finally, Gary Cantrell, better known as Lazarus Lake, founder of the Barkley Marathons held in Tennessee. I recently met him and shuttled him around as he walked through the Florida Panhandle towards the Gulf of Mexico. His walk began at Lake Michigan four months earlier. I have no clue how old Lazarus is, but I can tell you he's no spring chicken. His legs hurt, his feet were killing him, he must be north of seventy years old, but here he was walking across the country. It's never too late to chase a new dream.

I prayed and asked the Lord why I was almost forty before I felt called into trail ministry. After all, I had better knees and ankles when I was twenty. I knew the answer in my heart but thought it was worth the question. God simply confirmed what I knew to be true; I was nowhere near mature enough to handle this call at twenty years old. Looking back, I see how the Lord has shaped me, grown and matured me, and led me perfectly into what he had for me. Another reason is the trail itself. In the late 90s and early 2000s, thru-hiking had not taken off to the degree it is now. Twenty years ago, only a few hundred attempted a thru-hike of the Appalachian Trail. Today that number is in the thousands, with over two million setting foot on the trail for smaller hikes. This is a mission field that has grown over time. Amazingly, God set the harvesters up to be ready at the exact time the field came to full maturity.

What dream are you dreaming? This seems to be a running theme in this work. Someday I will open my own business, someday I will answer the call to preach, someday I will get my life together. Some day may be today, so wake up and realize today is your day! Age is an excuse, inexperience is an excuse, lack of time is an excuse. Let this lesson be a shock to your system, a pull into the unknown, a push to leave your comfort zone and chase your God-given dreams.

If it's truly important to you, you will find a way to make it work. I'm on a lot of hiking message boards. One question that gets asked over and over on these boards is, "how do you find time and have money to hike?" I always love to read creative answers, and I know people who've done them all. I met a hiker who worked as a dental hygienist for two years and slept in her car in the office parking lot to save money for her hike. Another sold his house, bought a tent, and started sleeping in the tent while working to save money. Almost everyone has sold stuff, shrunk their closets, minimalized their lives, and experienced difficulties to make their dreams of hiking a reality. It works the same for your dream. You might not be able to drive a 2022 model truck, might have to have a yard sale, perhaps a few sleepless nights, but if it's important, you find a way.

Any step toward your dream is a step in the right direction. For example, if you want to run a marathon, begin by walking to the mailbox. That might be all you can do, but if you walk to the mailbox, walk to the end of the road, then walk three miles. You get the picture; you must start taking steps in the right direction. I know people who have expressed dreams to me, but they have never taken a step in the direction of their dreams. Regardless of your age, if you start stepping in the right direction, you will be amazed at how far you will go. So, what if you never run the marathon. Maybe you run a couple 5K races, get more involved with the running community, or work the aid station at some big race; that beats sitting at the house and never getting involved at all.

Regret is a terrible thing. One of the biggest regrets of

those on their deathbed is they never chased their dreams and aspirations. They didn't dare to take the step. Choose to live your life in such a way that you die with your memories, not your dreams. I hate sounding like William Wallace trying to convince his army to fight England, but sometimes it takes someone a little fanatical to light a fire under a few people. True, if you chase your dreams, you may fail, you may break a hip, or you may lose some money. But if you don't, one day, you'll be lying on your deathbed wishing you could go back and have another opportunity to chase those dreams. Remember, a .300 batting average in a baseball career will almost certainly get you into the Hall of Fame, but that's hitting the ball three of every ten at-bats. You will miss sometimes, but you must be willing to swing. Regret, it is a terrible thing.

I once heard Bro. Vaudie Lambert preach a message entitled "One plus God." He talked of great men in the Bible who moved alone simply on the orders of the Lord and said no matter what you're up against, one plus God is a majority; it's an overwhelming force. We need to learn this lesson, if God has given you a dream, if he's called you, it doesn't matter what may come against you; he will see it through if you don't quit. What if he called you and you never got started? It's not too late to be used in some capacity. Trust in the Lord, lean on the Lord, it might be impossible in your current strength, but it's not impossible for him. It's not too late to chase that dream.

LESSON 23
WISDOM FROM THE MARGINS

How much better to get wisdom than gold!
And to get understanding is to be chosen
rather than silver.

— PROVERBS 16:16 NKJV

My mom ordered a new thin-lined preaching Bible about fifteen years ago for me, and when it came in, she realized that the Bible had become damaged during shipping. We discovered the inside cover had been ripped loose from the binding. The company instructed mom to destroy the Bible, but I wasn't having any of that. So I took the bible and duct-taped the spine to the front cover; in my opinion, this Bible was a perfect representation of how Jesus uses imperfect things for his purpose. In addition, it has a prayer map from Dr. Dick Eastman's ministry cut up and taped in the front and back covers. This takes you through praying for every nation on earth every thirty days. I have preached from this Bible for the last fifteen years, it has been to the tops of mountains, and I have written down every tidbit of wisdom I have heard preachers, evangelists, missionaries, say in the covers and margins for these fifteen years.

Here are some of my favorite bits of wisdom from the margins of my Bible; I hope they challenge and bless you, as they have me.

- Knowing God doesn't make us better than anyone else; it just makes us better than we were.
- Aspire to inspire before you expire
- When you're hanging on a low limb, you can still cry out to God. -Bro. Tom Towles
- God isn't looking for someone full of themselves. He's looking for someone full of him.
- We may be unworthy, but we aren't worthless.
- If you get people in front of the fire of God, it'll catch. -Jude Tharp
- Truth is more important than happiness
- Your discipline empowers you.
- The altar must be more than a piece of wood; it must be a lifestyle.
- The only bad prayer is no prayer.
- Faith is all I got. - Sis. Nellie Arnett
- Let my heart be broken by the things that

break God's heart. -Bob Pierce (World Vision Founder)

- Some of your most significant victories will be in the fights you never have.
- Talking about theory is always easier than doing something about the problem.
- A great awakening happens when the church, as usual, is not able to answer the questions posed by contemporary society. - Dr. David Copeland
- Success is not about being famous; it's about being faithful.
- All who perish are my parish. -John Wesley
- Simple obedience changes the world
- Today's priorities impact generations
- Obedience is God's love language.
- Jesus doesn't expect you to sit on your backside, perfecting doctrine. He expects you to work for him. - Brother Yun
- Knowledge of God does not equal intimacy with God
- If you want a new idea, read an old book.
- Lord, I want to see your power manifest uncommonly on common days.
- Brother, you stepped on my toes."
- I'm sorry, I was aiming for your heart."
- We need to move from a consumer mentality to a producer mentality.
- It's better to have a small wedding and a big

marriage than a big wedding and a small marriage.

- God requires you to go deep before you can go wide.
- We reproduce in others what we are.
- Straight is the way, narrow is the gate, and everybody is not going to like you.
- Elijah prayed a 63-word prayer, and fire fell from heaven. A short prayer will do just as good as a long prayer when you don't live far from heaven.
- Until you sure up your vertical relationship with the Lord, all your horizontal relationships with others will be a mess.
- Jesus didn't just share information. He shared love.
- The student with straight A's is irrelevant if the student with C's has more passion and persistence.
- Satan's masterpiece is the Pharisee, not the Prostitute.
- It doesn't matter if you speak in tongues when you are mean in English.
- A saved man believes in Jesus; a righteous man behaves like Jesus.
- Ministers fear God and the congregation members with the most money.
- The only thing worse than failing in the flesh is succeeding in it.
- Already and not yet

- Miracles happen at the edges.
- The American dream is to have it all; the Kingdom's call is to lose it all.
- Many people are in church but not in Christ. They grew up in church, but not in Christ.
- Speak words that rebuild the torn down places in others.
- Life isn't fair, but God is faithful.
- Our words are like Nitroglycerin; they can blow up bridges or heal hearts.
- God gives provision for your vision.
- It's easier to train faithful people to be talented than talented people to be faithful.
- You weren't born to make a living; you were born to make a difference.
- I'm not crazy. I just have a healthy disregard for the impossible.
- Busy isn't a virtue.
- We have too many cooks and not enough chefs. Cooks copy other recipes; Chefs create their own.
- Modern Christianity is focused on filling churches with people; the gospel is focused on filling people with God.
- It doesn't matter if you believe in Christ or not; sometime in the next hundred years, we will all meet him.
- Three things guide our lives:Pressures-what others want us to do, Pleasures-What you

want to do, Priorities- What God wants you
to do

- I'd rather believe God for a lot and get a little
than believe him for nothing and get it all
- My cause is greater than my camp.
- The closer you get to the cross, the smaller
the crowd. -T.F. Tenney
- It's every day, Bro.
- A divided nation is discouraging; a divided
church is devastating.
- It must be felt before it can be tell't. -Old
Mountain Saying
- We get uptight over things that don't
bother God.
- We compare what we know about ourselves to
what we don't know about others. It's our B roll
to their highlight reel. Don't make comparisons.
- We aren't Holy Ghost used car salesmen; we
plant, sow, water, and God gives the increase.
-Rev. John Coleman
- Your relationship with God was never meant
to revolve around buildings, systems, or
infrastructure.
- Pope Innocent III (boasting): No longer can
the church say silver and gold have I none.
- St. Francis of Assisi: True, but no longer does
the church have the power to say, "Rise and
Walk."
- If you want a man to build a ship, don't teach

him about wood and work; teach him to love
the ocean.

- Jesus shows up in unlikely places, with
unlikely people, and does unlikely things.

The Ship that Sails

I'd rather be the ship that sails
And rides the billows wild and free;
Than to be the ship that always fails
To leave its port and go to sea.
I'd rather feel the sting of strife,
Where gales are born and tempest roar;
Than to settle down to useless life
And rot in dry dock on the shore.
I'd rather fight some mighty wave
With honor in supreme command;
And fill at last a well-earned grave,
Than die in ease upon the sand.
I'd rather drive where sea storms blow,
And be the ship that always failed
To make the ports where it would go,
Than to be the ship that never sailed.

— ANONYMOUS

Notes

LESSON 6

1. Sjogren,Steve Conspiracy of Kindness: A Unique Approach to Sharing the Love of Jesus. Bloomington: Bethany House Publishers, 2003. Kindle Edition

LESSON 13

1. Garnett, M. *'Take Your Glory, Lord:' William Duma: His Life Story.* Roodepoort: Baptist Publishing House, 1980

LESSON 15

1. Charles, Templeton. Farewell to God: My Reasons for Rejecting the Christian Faith. McClelland & Stewart. 1996

LESSON 17

1. Brinkley D. *The Life and Times of Darrell Brinkley: Simple Life, Hard Work, Respect Others, Love of God and Country.* New York: Page Publishing, Inc. 2015
2. State of Food Insecurity and Nutrition in the nWorld 2020 online summary, http://www.fao.org/state-of-food-security-nutrition/en/
3. Milton, J. *Paradise Lost.* Penguin Classics, 2003.
4. Carnegie, D. *How to Stop Worrying and Start Living.* New York: Simon and Schuster, 1948.

LESSON 18

1. Bratton, S.P. *The Spirit of the Appalachian Trail: Community, Environment, and Belief on a Long-Distance Hiking Path*. Knoxville. University of Tennessee Press, 2015

LESSON 20

1. Olson, B. Bruchko. Charisma House, 1978.
2. Chan, S. *Evangelism in a Skeptical World: How to make the unbelievable news of Jesus more believable*. Grand Rapids: Zondervan. 2018

LESSON 21

1. http://www.summitpost.org/public-and-private-land-percentages-by-us-states/186111
2. Tolstoy, L., Lock, M., Maude, A., & Maude, L. *How Much Land Does A Man Need?* Brisbane, Qld. Locks' Press. 1986

ABOUT THE AUTHOR

Brad Sasser is currently the head of Trail Servants, a registered non-profit, ministering primarily to hikers and outdoor enthusiasts. He's been a Youth Pastor, Pastor, and currently a US Missionary. He, alongside his wife Michelle, and their two children, Lane (15) and Meredith (13) currently serves as a Chaplain. They travel the long trails of America showing the love of Christ to the hurting.

He holds a Bachelors degree in Social Science, an MBA with a concentration in accounting, and jokingly a PhD from the School of Hard Knocks. His greatest desire is to know the Lord and to make his love known among those in the outdoor communities of the world.

Instagram: @adventurepreacher **Facebook:** Brad Sasser
Email: trailservants@gmail.com
Download the free Trail Servants app on Apple or Google Play Stores

Lightning Source UK Ltd.
Milton Keynes UK
UKHW010154190322
400211UK00012B/336